(

# THE ALIENATED HERO IN
# MODERN FRENCH DRAMA

UNIVERSITY OF GEORGIA MONOGRAPHS, NO. 9

# The Alienated Hero

# in

# Modern French Drama

By
ROBERT EMMET JONES

PQ
558
.J6

UNIVERSITY OF GEORGIA PRESS
ATHENS                    1962

Copyright ©  1962
University  of  Georgia  Press
Library of Congress Catalog Card Number: 62-14239
Printed in the United States of America

# Contents

# Preface

THE choice of plays to be used in this study was a difficult one. There are few plays in the contemporary French theatre in which the leading character does not feel himself spiritually alienated from his fellow man, and there are almost as many in which he proclaims and bewails it loudly. An exhaustive study of this problem could easily run into volumes, with each dramatist being allotted at least one chapter, and some of them having whole books devoted to them.

I have chosen five types of alienated hero to study. Three of my chapters deal primarily with one author each because most of his plays treat similar subjects. Thus in discussing the heroines of Giraudoux it is neccessary to discuss his work as a whole because it deals with people, especially women, with ever similar problems. A similar technique has been used with the plays of Anouilh and Sartre. The aristocratic exiles and the characters of the lower depths are discussed with reference to several authors, because none has devoted, with the exception of Lenormand, whose work is now quite dated, the major part of his dramatic output to the problems of either.

My choices of plays were governed primarily by the importance of the author, as judged by leading French critics of the period, and secondly by the theme of alienation as found in modern plays.

Most contemporary critics agree that Giraudoux is one of the great figures of the contemporary theatre, and many critics also invariably place Anouilh, Montherlant, and Sartre in the front rank. The influence of Lenormand on the theatre of the twenties is undeniable, and he represents the concerns of this decade perhaps better than any other dramatist. There is no unanimity of choice as great as that which we find about the above-mentioned dramatists, although many modern critics have singular personal preferences. Although the backgrounds of the five men mentioned above differ in many respects, and although the years during which they wrote were years of great social and political changes which can be found echoed in their plays, a type of hero emerges from each of their works sufficiently similar to the heroes of each of the other dramatists to warrant his being treated with them in a single study.

I might have studied the role of the alienated hero in the dramas of Jean-Jacques Bernard, Gide, Vildrac, Bernstein, Cocteau, Amiel, Obey, Salacrou, Beckett, and many other playwrights whose works have appeared since the First World War. However, because of the necessity of limiting myself, I felt it would be more valuable to treat the alienation theme as it appeared in the works of major dramatists rather than in those of minor ones. The fact that the majority of the plays of Paul Claudel were written before or during the First World War eliminated from this study one of France's greatest dramatists.

I have studied *La Prisonnière* of Bourdet because it is the best known of the homosexual plays and *Un Taciturne* by Martin du Gard because I consider it to be the finest. I have chosen to study *Les Fossiles* of Curel, although it technically does not belong in the time span covered by this work, because it helps broaden the picture of the plight of the aristocrat in the modern world. This play serves as excellent contrast to the plays of Montherlant likewise concerned with aristocratic exiles.

The later plays of Anouilh are discussed only in passing because they are mainly repetitions of earlier works or mere broadenings of previously-used themes. The most important plays of Anouilh, I believe, are those written before and during the Second World War, and they, therefore, are the ones to which I devote most of my attention.

I should like to thank Professors Justin O'Brien, Jeanne Pleasants, and Bert Leefmans for the help which they gave me in an earlier version of this study. The encouragement given me by Professor Jules Alciatore and his wife, Audrey, has made it possible to complete this book. Their suggestions about the text and the interpretations of the plays have been invaluable. I should also like to thank Fred Bornhauser and Melvin Bentley for their suggestions and encouragement.

The translations in the text are my own except for those from Gide's *Journals*, which have been excellently translated by Justin O'Brien. Several other translations have been used, and they are mentioned in the footnotes.

R.E.J.

CHAPTER I

# Introduction: The Alienated Man
# As Tragic Hero

IN THE three decades following the First World War there appeared in France many dramatists whose plays elevated the quality of a theatre which from 1900 to 1920 had reached an almost unparalleled low point. It was during this period that the genius of Jean Giraudoux, Paul Claudel, Henri de Montherlant, and Jean Anouilh was first revealed. Lesser but still significant luminaries also appeared, for it was during these years that the talents of Albert Camus, Simone de Beauvoir, Edouard Bourdet, Henri-René Lenormand, François Mauriac, Roger Martin du Gard, Jean Cocteau, and Jean-Paul Sartre were developed.

Each of these playwrights wrote a twentieth-century equivalent of tragedy and helped restore serious drama to the place it had long since relinquished to other, lesser dramatic genres because of a dearth of great tragic dramatists. The work of these authors was uneven, poor plays appearing among the good ones with startling consistency, and yet most of these dramatists each produced one play which is a masterpiece. The best of them wrote several superior works, but none, with the exception of Claudel, Giraudoux, and Montherlant, produced a series of great plays in any way comparable to the successive masterpieces written by the dramatic giants Aeschylus, Sophocles, Euripides, Shakespeare, Racine, or even Musset or Ibsen.

There are several reasons for this inability to sustain a series of great dramatic productions, not the least important of which is the limited range of most of these writers, who, like Lenormand, Montherlant, and Anouilh, write about one person who seems to appear in each of the plays as a spokes-

1

man for the author or, like Sartre, Camus, Bourdet, and Giraudoux, write about the same types of people with ever similar problems.

Many of the heroes and heroines of Anouilh seem to be the same character in varying circumstances. In his comedies and tragedies the backgrounds of his characters, their reactions to life, and their actions in life are all surprisingly alike and perhaps identical with those of their creator. Their follies, vices, and virtues all show such remarkable resemblances that it is quite possible to remove a hero from one play and transfer him to another without changing the plot of the second play at all.

In the plays of Giraudoux the heroines are like sisters who serve the same functions in different contexts. They are all chosen individuals, *chosen* to serve both God and man and to set right the ways of a corrupted world. They are all essentially virginal, and their conflicts with corruption, authority, or superstition emphasize the conflicts of modern man. One could continue to cite indefinitely examples of this seeming inability on the part of contemporary French dramatists to create any great range of characters, but further examples will be postponed to later stages of the discussion.

Another reason for the failure of contemporary dramatists to broaden the scope of their works may be their tendency to cater to the taste of their public and the critics, who, too often, prefer insignificant and frothy plays to serious ones with tragic implications. When the creation of a trivial work brings an author more money, he may be tempted to continue writing in the manner for which his public is willing to pay.

In the three decades following the First World War, tragedy was neither the most popular form of dramatic art nor, when it was good, did it always succeed for the reason good tragedy should succeed, that is, because it is good tragedy. Not a little of the success of Lenormand in France, or in America of Eugene O'Neill, was due to their experimentation, to their ability to stimulate the jaded appetites of the curious, pleasure-seeking public of the nineteen-twenties with bizarre stage effects such as O'Neill's use of tom-toms in *The Emperor Jones* or by the then novel theatrical portrayals of sexual anomaly.

In these three decades Giraudoux, Anouilh, and Martin du Gard received more adulation for their comedies than for their tragedies, and Giraudoux's tragedies, fine as they are, were seldom successful in their original productions.

The popular successes in this period were the musicals, the extravaganzas, the farces, the bedroom comedies, and the melodramas. The public seemed to want a theatre of escape which would make it forget the economic and political catastrophes too much a part of daily life. Witness for example the number of performances given to *Judith* (about one hundred) as compared to the performances of the works of Sacha Guitry which often ran for years. The average playgoer could lose himself for several hours in the midst of light music, colorful costumes, and bawdy humor, but he seemed unable to do so while witnessing tragedy. Tragedy should provide the spectator an emotional purge, but it has not often been able to do so in our day perhaps because the serious playwrights have too long been preoccupied with writing *tranches de vie*. The average playgoer of the contemporary period has probably preferred visiting mental institutions or the brothels of Montmartre to seeing them depicted on the stage. Little of the nobility of man could be found there, in any case, and depression or, worse, boredom, was the audience's ultimate reaction to these plays.

It was not until after 1920 that the dramatist again tried to assume the mantle of tragedy and to revive interest in an art form which had appeared moribund to many people. Dramatists in general, however, were unable or unwilling to throw off the double yoke of Ibsenism and naturalism. Only the greatest learned something from the naturalists, assimilated it, and then proceeded to develop their own ideas. The large majority, however, wrote thesis plays and dramas with social messages, plays of discontent which only aroused more discontent and might as well have been comic operas as tragedies. Traces of this naturalistic theatre are found in the early plays of Lenormand and Anouilh, in many of Sartre's plays, and in several plays by Bourdet.

Other playwrights sought to remove all naturalistic influences from their works, and many of them ended in a realm of non-communication or, at best, of partial communication. Playwrights like Gantillon, Pellerin, and Cocteau often carried their experiments too far and were at as great a distance from attaining tragedy as had been the naturalists.

Both groups of playwrights, the naturalists and the experimentalists, produced some interesting plays, in some instances even good ones, but neither of them produced great tragedy. It is a third group, those playwrights who not only assimilated ideas and techniques from the past and experimented in their own right, but who also sought to create tragedy, or something approximating it, for our day, with which I shall be concerned in this study.

Even the most casual reading of the plays written and produced since 1920 indicates that isolation is one of the most important themes, if not the essential one, of modern drama. The heroes and heroines of almost all the major French playwrights of this period are subjected—by themselves or by society—to exile from the cotidian world. Often this alienation is forced upon them because of their inability to adjust to the conventions of society; often they force themselves to become exiles because they will not accept (as distinguished from *cannot* accept) the laws and conventions which make an orderly if mediocre world.

Since the age of heroes has long ago passed and now survives only in the texts of a few epic poems and tragedies that have come down to us from antiquity or from the more recent but aesthetically equal distance of the two great ages of modern drama, the Elizabethan and the French seventeenth century, man has resigned himself to his insignificance in a world which is unaware of him or else hostile to him. That there are men and women who will not accept this position is evidenced by the modern theatre peopled with exiles whose creators have tried to make of them tragic heroes. Their tragedies, however, have only one meaning for us, namely, that there is no such thing as Aristotelian tragedy in the contemporary theatre because we, having lost our faith in man, as well as in God, as Joseph Wood Krutch says,[1] think they are either ridiculous for attempting to appear tragic or noble, or else that they are uninstructed fools who are trying to impress us with their own dexterity.

Mr. Krutch, in his *The Modern Temper*, places in focus the reasons why he believes tragedy, in its classic sense, cannot be written today:

If the plays and novels of today deal with little people and less mighty emotions it is not because we have become interested in commonplace souls and their unglamourous adventures, but because we have come, willy-nilly, to see the soul of man as com-monplace and its emotions as mean.[2]

He continues, saying that the idea of nobility is inseparable from the idea of tragedy which cannot exist without it, that tragedy is essentially an expression, not of despair, but of triumph over despair and of confidence in the value of human life. "Hence it is," he goes on, "that tragedy, however tre-mendous it may be, is an affirmation of faith in life, a declara-tion that even if God is not in his heaven, then at least Man is in his world. We accept the outward defeats which it describes for the sake of the inward victories which it reveals."[3]

Tragedy gives a meaning, a justification, to the universe, and the tragic author, even if he does not believe in God, must have faith in man. Our society, says Mr. Krutch, is too sophisticated.[4] It distrusts its own thought, it despises its own passions, and it realizes its unimportance in the universe. Its heroes cannot therefore be noble or even significant. Every-thing becomes merely absurd.

Shakespeare justifies the ways of God to man, but in Ibsen there is no such happy end and with him tragedy, so-called, has become merely an expression of our despair at finding that such justification is no longer possible.[5]

But the authors of our day continue to write tragedy, so-called, and continue to try to see some nobility in man.

The purpose of this book is not primarily to judge whether tragedy has been written recently. It is rather to discuss the role of the alienated hero in modern serious drama and the extent to which he dominates the contemporary French theatre. But the problem of tragedy must be touched on because the exiles of the theatre of today are considered by the public and by many critics to be that theatre's tragic heroes and heroines.

Certainly these heroes are a new and different group of characters who, when placed beside their predecessors in the dramatic hierarchy, immediately pale. They are a generation of sick people when compared with the characters of Shake-speare or Sophocles. The strength of an Oedipus, a Macbeth, an Electra is seldom found in these modern plays.

In the great tragedies of Sophocles, Euripides, Aeschylus, Shakespeare, and Racine the protagonists are heroes who differ from other men not only because of their social rank but also because of their superior moral and intellectual strength. Some great passion such as Oedipus' pride or Macbeth's ambition or Phèdre's guilty love may make its possessor different from other men and actually may alienate him from society. This feeling of difference, however, does not become an obsession with him as it does with our contemporary dramatis personae. All tragic heroes are exiled morally or spiritually from their contemporaries; one has only to remember the heroes and heroines in our dramatic heritage to be convinced of this. Each hero in tragic literature rejects his society or is rejected by it. This does not mean, however, that he will ignore the rejectors. He acts and either tries to ameliorate the very society which has no place for him or proves that in rejection one can still retain his integral nobility of character. Few tragic heroes disintegrate as a result of their conflicts with others without first having proved that man's possibilities are great, in short that life is worth living. It is these heroes who give meaning to life, heroes from whom we can learn much about human nature. In this respect they transcend their times and become universal, because human nature remains essentially the same throughout the centuries.

In the modern drama the hero differs from other men either because he despises them or because he is completely unconcerned with them, so obsessed is he with his own problems. Few of these modern heroes are distinguished by admirable moral or intellectual qualities; and thus we fail to respect them, because they are self-centered and eccentric, as most classic heroes are not. Among these modern heroes are found homosexuals, decaying aristocrats, sadists, psychotics, and naive young girls. Some of them are not accepted by the society into which they were born; others renounce that society. In either case they become alienated from what our sociologists might call a well-adjusted contemporary existence. All of these heroes feel their loneliness: they vociferously reiterate at all possible moments their sense of solitude, and yet most of them encourage that solitude by being distinctly anti-social. Because there is little constructive in their attitude towards life, it is not surprising that society will have little to do with them. It does not seem strange therefore that we learn little of the greatness of man from them although we do learn much about the social group which casts them aside.

And the modern drama, it might be said, becomes a commentary on the modern world, but only an extensive footnote in the book of human nature.

Perhaps the most notable difference between the heroes of the classic playwrights and those of our contemporary dramatists is the reaction of the two types of men to their destiny, their awareness of their own problems and those of mankind in general. The hero of Sophocles will meet his destiny, will become aware of himself and accept the consequences of his actions. He will have learned something in the course of the play. At the same time he sees that there is something in life more important than himself, to which he is willing to sacrifice himself or let himself be sacrificed.

For the most part, the modern heroes run and hide from their destinies. If they do become aware of themselves, and few of them do, they will more often than not plead with and cajole an unsympathetic society. They will seldom meet the consequences of their own acts; they will seldom even admit them. They have learned little, if anything, in the course of a play, and we, the spectators, have learned even less. The modern hero generally seems impotent to act because he does not believe that there is anything in life worth saving. When he does act his action seems a futile one because he destroys, it appears too often, for the salvation neither of his contemporaries nor even of himself, but rather for the very sake of destruction. Psychotic King Ferrante of *La Reine Morte* or the neurotic Thérèse of *La Sauvage* or the frustrated Thierry of *Un Taciturne* or the Luc de Brontë of *Le Mangeur de rêves* become therefore merely case histories, and these characters are among the best that our playwrights offer. Their creators intend them to be, if not tragic, at least meaningful. They are certainly not tragic, and their meaning is a limited one. I hope to demonstrate in this study that in an effort to portray some sort of tragic figure the modern dramatist has created a race of unadmirable exiles who seem devoid of tragic significance because they are seldom of our world. And the modern theatre, consequently, appears to be an attack on environment rather than a defense of the universe, or an attack on man rather than a demonstration of his occasional majesty and importance.

When the audience of Shakespeare's day or of Sophocles' era viewed a play they knew that both they and the characters they were witnessing in action had dignity and a place in the general order of things. The viewer was not alone. The creator of the drama he was seeing was concerned with universal values, with justifying man and his world to man. It was this unity of human experience and the basic similarities of men which they were portraying. And this was more or less accepted as the work of the dramatist until the nineteenth century.

The romantic invasion unwittingly and certainly unwillingly prohibited the treatment of man as a noble being. With the romantics the differences among men mattered much. The ego, the eccentric became emphasized in literature. And yet the romantics, too, tried to see nature in grandiose terms. They comforted themselves and each other with the assurance that nature complemented them, reflected their moods, in short, that they, too, had a place in the general order of the world, as their predecessors had had. But there was a difference. They looked upon themselves and their own emotions as being the things which mattered most in life. Their art became personal expression, and although their lyric poetry was among the greatest the world had ever known, they could not create stage characters except in their own image. The Byronic characters, Cain, Manfred, Marino Faliero, were all Byron posing, just as the dramatis personae of Hugo were offshoots of his titanic personality. These heroes often caught the fancy of the public (Hugo's still do) but few of them are especially great creations. If the romantic plays are staged today, it is because the majesty and sweep of their poetry make them still appealing. The nineteenth century was not an age of great drama.

The egocentric and eccentric characteristics of the heroes of the romantic drama become quite evident upon reading that theatre. Manfred and Cain, like Dumas' Antony, are egotists who, aside from partaking of some secret sin which sets them apart from their contemporaries, are alienated from a society which they despise. Hernani is a bandit and Ruy Blas a hired upstart. Both live precariously on the outskirts of society. They are noble men, to be sure, but they are self-centered and are subject to an interior exile which sets them off from their more vicious fellow men and inadvertently leads to their ultimate and meaningless deaths. Chatterton, the eccentric young poet whom society does not accept, and whose very sensitivity is the cause of his death, is but another example of a romantic hero spiritually alienated from his fellow man. And his death is not tragic in the sense that Hamlet's death is tragic because, accomplishing nothing, it has no meaning. It is but an attack on the society which turned him away. In similar fashion the ruin of Marguerite Gautier, Olympe, and Paula Tanqueray, all women of easy virtue, is an attack on the society which bore them rather than a justification of their existence. A catalogue of nineteenth-century heroes and heroines alienated from their society could be continued indefinitely, and examples could be added from the works of Chateaubriand, the epic poems of Lamartine, the poetry and novels of Vigny, and the novels of Hugo and Stendhal. The whole romantic period was concerned with the plight of the superior man who seemed doomed to a life of isolation. What is remarkable, however, is that the emphasis is more on the blackness of the society which has rejected these heroes than on the tragedy of the heroes themselves. Mankind in nineteenth-century drama is usually painted black; the heroes are generally whitewashed—their sins are not their own but the fault of their society. In the classic drama established order and the alienated hero are varying shades of gray.

I should like to suggest that the heroes and heroines of the serious plays of today are the spiritual brothers and sisters of the dramatis personae of the nineteenth-century romantic plays, that they are siblings—but with a difference. They are creations still further removed, in most cases, from the ideal of the tragic hero, than are their romantic counterparts. In many instances their creators have exiled them from their contemporaries for far more damning reasons—homosexuality, thievery, prostitution—than the authors of the romantic plays exiled their characters. Many of the heroes and heroines of today seem to be unwholesome people whose need for help, psychological and otherwise, should have been obvious since their childhood. Too often there is little attractive about them. And so our plays tend to appear to be mostly clinical histories of maladjusted people who are lost in a world that does not understand them because they do not understand themselves. Their egocentricity and eccentricities ally them with the romantics; their overt sexual and psychiatric disorders identify them with the post-Freudian era.

Characters who in the Greek world would have been

treated as mean and probably as comic have become the subjects of so-called tragedy in the modern theatre. The sexual deviant who is just a homosexual, the ignorant racial exile who has nothing more than the problem of miscegenation to make him interesting, the vulgar lower middle-class characters of Anouilh or of Arthur Miller in America, the psychiatric cases of Lenormand, and the egotists of Montherlant might well have been treated as comic characters by a Greek dramatist.

Ours, however, is an age of difference, an age, perhaps, of social consciousness where every man can stand alone, and to poke fun at one who is different is, among the educated groups, social suicide. Before one can satirize or mock another, one is expected to delve into his sociological, psychological, and psychiatric background and then attempt to understand him. Tragedy, however, cannot be written about misfits. Misfits are the subject of comedy, and yet our comic authors avoid writing about them. And so they are made the subject of what in our days passes for tragedy.

If we accept the fact that the protagonists of our drama are the spiritual relatives of the heroes of the nineteenth-century drama, we might almost say that today's theatre is a culmination of the romantic, that its themes, essentially the same, have been broadened to include almost anything which appears in the author's mind, that its characters are as egocentric and eccentric as those of the last century, that even its outlook is basically romantic and adolescent, and that the effects which it achieves, its feeling of confusion and despair, are exactly the same.

What the romantics could not say, or dared not say—that Manfred was a repressed homosexual, that courtesans could be common prostitutes, that impotency was impotency and not just a general feeling of malaise—the moderns have said. They have gone one step further than the romantics.

The modern themes which were just hinted at in nineteenth-century drama are outgrowths mainly of the liberties taken by the naturalistic theatre of the turn of the century and by the twentieth-century novel which has led the way toward enlarging man's knowledge of man. But in the theatre this enlargement is one of breadth rather than of depth. The wealth of subject matter has been extended, but there have been few major dramatic characters created from it. We may now be more aware of certain aspects of life, formerly hidden in deference to public opinion, than were our grand-fathers, but we do not understand them or mankind the more just by the fact of their having been presented to us. Were they presented to us as adjuncts or major characters of tragic figures whom we could somehow admire and understand, then perhaps we might be justified in saying that the modern drama has given us the depth of which many critics think it is no longer capable.

It might be argued that the novel, designed for a different audience and employing means different from those of the drama, can treat problems which seem more effectively con-temporary. To this one might answer that Oedipus and Hamlet and many other tragic figures are as great as, if not greater than, the creations found even in the finest novels. The medium is unimportant; it is with the creator that the re-sponsibility for the creation lies. And if in our world the finer tragic creations seem to be found in novels then we might say that the writers with the greatest comprehension of tragedy have been more concerned with fiction than with drama, or perhaps that they have found fiction more congenial for the creation of tragic characters.

## Chapter II

# The Aristocrat

The nobleman has been obsolete for a century and a half. Time has stopped for him. It stopped for his family and peers several generations before he was born. Meanwhile the world has progressed and forgotten about him or, at best, regarded him as a curiosity and an anachronism. The era of revolutions had taken his wealth, his social standing, and often his life. He became an exile looking in on the world of the lower and middle classes, but he looked through a glass darkly, unaware of his faulty vision; and when he tried to become a part of their world, he could not do so either because pride forbade it or because the world would not permit it. He was still a man, but he was an impotent social animal.

The plight of the nobleman should have appealed as subject matter to the dramatists of the nineteenth and twentieth centuries because in his dilemma may be found the seeds of tragedy. The modern dramatist, however, in his search for new forms and novel subject matter has bypassed the nobleman and concentrated his art upon the problems of the lower and middle classes, on plays with a message for a specific group of people. In a world in which personal tragedy appears to have become commonplace and uninteresting, the dramatic author can evoke only a certain amount of pity when he writes of an inferior or an equal of ours—witness Willy Loman in *Death of a Salesman*. Furthermore, since in our modern democratic age we feel, or are constantly told that we should feel, that we have no social superiors, the problems of a man of aristocratic birth become almost meaningless to us. And yet such men provide a commentary of great importance upon modern life, as I shall attempt to demonstrate when I speak of the several plays which do deal with his plight.

It is in the novel that the aristocrat has been treated as a

truly tragic figure. In a long series of books from Stendhal's
*Armance* to Proust's *A la Recherche du temps perdu* and
Montherlant's *Les Célibataires* he has been shown in different garbs under varying circumstances, all of them essentially tragic. Among these representatives of a dying culture
Edith Wharton in *The Age of Innocence*, Henry James in a
large part of his work, and Faulkner, too, have found tragedy.
But in the theatre, the consecrated medium for tragedy, the
aristocrat has seldom found his place.

To be sure, he has been treated by social satirists and comic
playwrights such as Chekhov, Wilde, Lavedan, and Bourdet,
but these authors seem only to point up his eccentricities and
vices (with slight nostalgia on the author's part for the former
"glory" of the nobleman, and often with a tinge of jealousy).
Furthermore, these authors have seldom really penetrated their
subject, have seldom "felt themselves into his skin." They have
treated him from the outside as an amusing phenomenon good
for a sneer or a chuckle; seldom have they treated him as a
human being. This was not their object, of course. Wilde
wanted to amuse and to be thought brilliant, and he suc-
ceeded. His comedies, however, are not noted for their
depth or subtle characterization. They are comedies of words
where plot and character are subservient to the dialogue,
and as such they throw little light on the problems of the
aristocrat.

Bourdet is more merciless in his satire than Wilde. His
social comedies—and especially *La Fleur des pois*—have tragic
overtones. But what he sees are the vices of the aristocracy,
its snobbery, its sexual disorders, its immorality, its complete
emphasis on self at the expense of others. He does not show
the reasons for these vices nor, as a comic writer, is he concerned with them. He is more interested in portraying social
fossils in a degenerate atmosphere, and, to make the portrait
more colorful, he paints a slightly distorted picture of them.
He does this well. But he, too, has not presented us with the
tragedy of the nobleman.

Before the plays of Montherlant were produced in Paris in
the nineteen-forties, there was produced successfully in France
only one play with tragic overtones, of which the subject
matter was the plight of the aristocrat in the modern world.
This play, *Les Fossiles* by François de Curel, an aristocrat
whose family had been prominent since the Crusades, was

written in 1892 and, although it achieved some success in the early years of this century, it is now a museum piece, a fossil like those it describes. As a sociological tract the play is most impressive, and the poetic dialogue often rises to heights of great lyric beauty, but the sterility and shallowness of the characters contribute toward making the play a failure.

*Les Fossiles* depicts the attempts of an old and very aristocratic family to produce an heir who will carry on the family name. Robert de Chantemelle, the dying son, is the only member of the clan who is able to make a compromise between the past, present, and future. The other members of the family—the Duc de Chantemelle, Robert's father, interested only in family succession; Claire, his daughter, who is too Cornelian in her devotion to duty and honor to be entirely credible; the Duchesse de Chantemelle, whose chief characteristic is her patience with the other members of the family—live essentially in the past and only seldom complain about their plight as social fossils.

Claire expresses the sentiments of the family when she speaks of her ancestors and the fact that with Robert's death the line will become extinct:

Certainly I understand! . . . (*becoming more and more carried away as she speaks*) The dukes of Chantemelle! They are on every page of the history of France! . . . It's frightful that Robert should be so close to death, but to think that after him, all our glorious past, that almost royal grandeur, will be no more than a memory! . . .[1]

Parallel with this colossal pride is another sentiment which runs through the play as a persistent overtone. Each member of the family, with the exception of the Duke, realizes that he is a fossil who does not really belong in the twentieth century. Quite often a sense of desperation makes the characters, almost involuntarily, revolt verbally against this condition. The Duchess, speaking with Claire, expresses this revolt:

Your father and you are like that . . . and Robert, too. You live in the past which acclaimed us without understanding how much the present forgets us. The times have changed so! Ah! the Duke of Chantemelle can become extinct. He will leave no gap, none, do you see . . . (*She sobs.*) except in his mother's heart.[2]

Robert is torn between the past and the present. His heart is in the past but his intellect places him among his contemporaries, and it is this characteristic which distinguishes and also alienates him from his family as well as from his middle-class contemporaries. He tells Claire that with his fellow students he becomes:

. . . more authoritarian than papa, more religious than mama, more royalist than you. The truth is that there are people who are out of place at the top of the social ladder as well as at the bottom. I am one of these. My own century claims my mind; the past claims my heart! Wherever I go it is exile for half of myself. My son must be saved from this torture.[3]

A young girl who has been staying with the family has become pregnant, and Robert marries her. She bears a son who will carry on the family name. One is never quite sure whose child she has, Robert's or his father's, for Hélène has had relations with both of them. The immorality of this situation, which links *Les Fossiles* to the *théâtre rosse*, is overlooked by several in the family since the infant in either case is the future Duke of Chantemelle.

The Duke is the most cruelly condemned character in the play. Because his sole interest appears to be the transmission of the family name, he is rebuked by the Duchess who, at the same time, damns the whole race of noblemen:

The child! . . . How artlessly you say that word! . . . If the poorest of our peasants loses his son he weeps for him. Robert dies and you weep for a title! . . . And not even that! The title is saved![4]

The salvation of his social group is seen by Robert, however. The fifth act of the play contains his precepts (and Curel's undoubtedly) for the role which the aristocrat should play in the modern world. These precepts are to be given to his son when he reaches maturity:

When little Henri reaches the age of fifteen, I authorize Hélène to settle with him in Paris and seek the educational resources that one finds only there. The future Duke of Chantemelle must be reared with the conviction that his rank does not exempt him from having personal merit. Let nothing be neglected in making of him in the strictest sense of the word a modern man. Let him love his own times and understand their greatness. We are wasted in carrying on the hatred, quite legitimate while the blood spilled by the Revolution was still bright, but which will soon serve only to disguise a debasing tendency towards selfishness and idleness. Under the pretext that the Revolution guillotined our grandparents who, at first, were enthusiastic about it, let us not remain hostile to all social progress. On the contrary, let us remain in the tradition by paying for our noble errors with our lives, and by so doing affirming the duty of the nobility to be a school of impartiality, showing the way to its century, audacious of mind and dupe of the heart! When the unfortunate and the humble lay claim to a larger place in the sun, let us know how to march at their head with enough scepticism to say to ourselves that our own troops will shoot us in the back. That is a good way for us to die. It seems to me that the nobility has had its day. Its ranks have been swelled too much by gold, too little by talent. It has always been closed to eminent men sent to it by the commoners, and in its turn the commoners are closed to it. Before it disappears, its last representatives, by a pious illusion, must leave the same impression of grandeur as the gigantic fossils which make one dream of ages long gone by.[5]

Written as a play of ideas, and actually a rather beautiful elegy on the death of the nobility, *Les Fossiles* is not the tragedy of one man, but rather the tragedy of time and social change, the tragedy of a special group. There is, however, no social conflict in Curel's play. We see the nobleman *chez lui* but never in contact with life itself. His problem, in terms of tragedy, therefore, has little meaning for us.

In Tennessee Williams' *A Streetcar Named Desire*, a play which when produced in France in 1950 had no little effect, the aristocrat is seen in conflict with the contemporary world, and from this conflict emerges a play which is closer to tragedy than *Les Fossiles*. The Civil War was as destructive to the Southern aristocracy as the French Revolution had been to the French nobility. Where once had been a rigid social system based on slavery and ruled by the cultured, wealthy aristocrats, there was after the Civil War complete anarchy and loss of values. When the economic system on which this society had been based was destroyed, the society itself fell with it.

When his plantation was broken up, the Southern aristocrat was faced with three alternatives. He could accept the changes the war had made and conform to the new society; he could migrate west and start again; or he could retire from active life in the new South, live in a world of false values, and become completely alienated from the society which he sired unknowingly and which had rejected him. The proudest (and the weakest, perhaps) chose the last way; it was certainly the easiest. But, as the years rolled by, this group, still retaining its pre-war viewpoint and ignoring everyone who was not acceptable by *ante-bellum* standards, steadily degenerated.[6]

*Les Fossiles* shows the stagnation of a family of the nobility and its tendency toward disintegration. *A Streetcar Named Desire* shows what has happened after the disintegration has set in. In it we have the aristocrat in contact with modern life, fighting a negative battle which can only end in failure. At the end of each play the aristocrats are still exiles, but there is an element of hope in *Les Fossiles*. Robert's precepts for his son save the play from being one of complete despair. There is only despair at the end of Williams' play, relieved only partially by the fact that one of the characters, Stella, an aristocrat, has made the compromise with modern life. The life which she chooses, however, is hardly edifying.

Henri de Montherlant also portrays the aristocrat in his theatre but his aristocrats differ from those of Curel and Williams. Finding greatness of spirit lacking in the modern world, Montherlant portrays men of noble birth, who lived in earlier ages, who are also men of great power. To these men, Ferrante in *La Reine morte*, Alvaro in *Le Maître de Santiago*, and Malatesta, he gives traits which esthetically seem characteristic of men of former times, the age of heroes, but he also places them in a type of spiritual isolation which is characteristic of contemporary literature. Montherlant undoubtedly chose his heroes from earlier historical epochs because there the nobleman had his place in society, and if his heroes have renounced that society it is only because they cannot tolerate the mediocrity which seems so apparent in it.

The heroes of the drama of Montherlant, however, including Georges Carrion of *Fils de personne* and L'Abbé de Pradts of *La Ville dont le prince est un enfant*, are all men who come into contact with problems which are common to the twentieth century. All of these heroes of Montherlant are exiles because they are superior individuals who will not adjust to or accept the society of which they are a part. Their outrageous sense of superiority to anything beyond themselves forbids them this adjustment. Like the heroes of Anouilh, they must have all or nothing, but their colossal egos and eccentric views of human nature will not permit them to accept life on its own terms and hence their loneliness. Ferrante and Malatesta have such tremendous confidence in their own superiority that they not only mistrust but also scorn the people who surround them. Alvaro's pride forces him to retire from a world in which the nobility of the human spirit has been replaced by greed and hypocrisy. Georges Carrion despises mediocrity and, because he feels his son is mediocre like so many people of his time, turns the young boy away. The Abbé de Pradts wants to refuse a world in which his pure love for one of his students is not tolerated.[7]

Pierre-Henri Simon finds that in Montherlant's theatre there is "une morale de qualité" which consists of:

. . . the isolation of the superior individual, scorn of people, hatred of sentimentality, refusal of social obligations, all that, in the last analysis, founded on a desperate view of man's fate. . . .[8]

These characteristics of Montherlant's theatre show only too well the state of alienation in which his aristocrats of mind as well as birth find themselves. None of these aristocrats is alienated because society had imposed this status upon him. Each is a self-made exile, a man who refuses life in society because society does not live up to his individual standards.

Ferrante, the first of Montherlant's aristocratic heroes, is a man who lives in solitude. He despises his son because Pedro is not a superior man. His advisors and ministers are alien to him.[9] He is, because he chooses to be, alone. He is a pessimist who has no confidence in human nature. He is convinced that everyone in his court is hypocritical, and that sooner or later all men become hypocrites. His unflattering estimate of man is expressed quite clearly when he says, "People always say that the butterfly comes from a worm; with man it's the butterfly that becomes a worm."[10] If this is not black romanticism as we find it in the drama of Anouilh it certainly is the exaggeration of several of the tenets dear to the hearts of Wordsworth and his circle to whom, alas, the child is father to the man. But whereas to Wordsworth this fact was cause for pity, to Montherlant it is cause for contempt. The difference lies in the subtle changes of mind which men have experienced in the last hundred and fifty years.

The only person in whom Ferrante has any faith is himself, and he often wonders whether he should place faith even there. Could this not arise from the fact that Ferrante is an inconsistent person whose only coherence is in his own inconsistency?[11] He acts on the spur of the moment according to his moods. He never quite knows what he wants or what he should do. In fact, the only thing which appears certain to him is that he is tired of his throne, tired of life, and awaiting death.

Ferrante's son, Pedro, has married, unknown to his father, Inès de Castro, who is now expecting the birth of his child. The king is furious when he discovers the marriage and mocks Pedro's avowals of love for his wife. When Pedro informs him that only Inès can make him happy, the king reacts in such a way as to show how horrible his own solitude must be:

Happier! Happiness again, like the other! It's an obsession! Do I worry about being happy?[12]

Ferrante is never happy. He is resigned to his status as king and to the solitude which accompanies it. He cannot understand the happiness of others especially when that happiness is the product of a mediocrity which he despises. Yet his jealousy of his son's happiness is partially the cause of his having Inès executed. Ferrante is not quite sure why he orders Inès' death. Pierre-Henri Simon feels that he commits this act because she has heard and understood the confession of his own despair.[13] This is undoubtedly one of the reasons, but there appear to be two others which bear equal weight. Ferrante, like all of Montherlant's heroes, is unhappy and solitary. He senses his isolation strongly and the mere appearance of love and happiness in others causes him feelings of resentment and jealousy. If he cannot have happiness why should others have it? They should not, he assures himself, and then executes Inès. The other reason for Ferrante's precipitate decision is his awareness that death is approaching. Before he dies he wants to commit an act by which he can show his courtiers that he still is king.[14] The outrageous nature of the act obviously makes it the more impressive both to himself and to his court, and nothing seems more stimulating to Ferrante than impressing himself with his own power.

Ferrante realizes that his isolation has made of him a sick man. He tells Inès, "Like me, you, too, are sick."[15] Her malady, he claims, is hope, which he cannot understand. His malady, which he does not state, is his lack of hope and confidence in the value of human life. His killing Inès is a monstrous act and he realizes it: "The more I calculate the injustice and atrociousness of what I do, the more I plunge into it, because it gives me the more pleasure."[16]

It should be obvious from this quotation that combined with his haughty aloofness from the world is a streak of sadism which permits Ferrante to exercise his power.

Yet he realizes that one can never escape from an act once one has committed it, and in this idea he joins the heroes of Anouilh and Sartre:

Of course. The tragedy of acts. An act is nothing at the moment. It is an object that you throw in the river. But it follows the course of the river, it is still there, in the distance, quite in the distance, always there; it passes through country after country; one finds it when he is no longer thinking of it, when he least expects it. Is this interminable existence of acts fair? I think not. But there it is.[17]

If one cannot free himself from his acts, as Ferrante says in this passage, the King must realize when he condemns Inès that he will eventually have to account for it. Being near death, he seems rather foolhardy in committing such an act, but perhaps his egotism is asserting itself in a defiance of God as well as of man.

Alvaro, the leading character of *Le Maître de Santiago*, is, like Ferrante, a proud and lonely man. Ferrante, however, being King of Portugal, must come into contact with his subjects. Alvaro is completely isolated from the outside world. The only thing which is real to him is, as his daughter Mariana says, what passes through his mind.[18] He has refused his world because he finds it to be a place where honor is no longer respected. He is therefore only too pleased to have been forgotten by a country in which he once shone as a national hero and an honorable gentleman:

It is an honor to be forgotten by an epoch like ours; perfect contempt likes to be held in contempt by what it holds in contempt in order to find itself justified.[19]

Alvaro has said no to his epoch much as the heroes and heroines of Anouilh and Giraudoux say no to theirs. His withdrawal from the world emphasizes his position of self-imposed exile. To combat his dislike of men and of his epoch Alvaro has turned to God. His life has become one of contemplation because for him humanity no longer exists. His callousness towards his daughter stems from this rejection of man as does his denial of the right of others to be happy, a denial reminiscent of Ferrante and Georges Carrion.

But, much like Créon, in Anouilh's *Antigone*, who defends in a more debasing manner, perhaps, the necessity of accepting life and working within its confines, one of the other members of the order of Santiago, Vargas, tells the remaining members of the group that one can be just as heroic in accepting life as in denying it:

Let's accept the fact that it is heroism to consent to be all alone through faithfulness to one's ideas. Wouldn't it also be heroism to play your part in a society that offends you so that in it you can make prevail those ideas which, if they are not incarnated, will remain more or less impotent?[20]

Alvaro will not be swayed by this argument and his attitude remains profoundly negative. This negation is actually the easiest solution, as another member of the order suggests:

And besides, what is humanly fine is not affecting a lofty manner but rather adapting oneself; it is not fleeing to be virtuous at one's ease, it is being virtuous in the world where difficulties are.[21]

Alvaro, as is made more than evident, is a pessimist. Like Ferrante, he feels that there is little good in man. He claims that nobility of spirit is always defeated; history is the story of its renewed defeats.[22] Because of this unalterable fact he believes that the only solution for his problem is to prepare himself for death by contemplating the deity. Man must be avoided, because "Every human being is an obstacle for him who strains for God."[23]

Another element of Alvaro's character which is common to all the Montherlant heroes is his immense egotism and pride. He claims that he is the man that all men should be.[24] Bernal, another of the members of the rapidly disappearing order, understands Alvaro's immense pride but criticizes him for it:

Bernal: You cannot force everyone to be satisfied with an absolute which is only made for some people.
Alvaro: I tolerate only perfection.[25]

This egotism is the direct cause of his alienation because through his misguided attempts at self-perfection and his consequent denial of the worth of anyone less perfect than he, he is negating life and the truth of the Christian belief that all men are imperfect.

As in *La Reine morte*, there are grotesque overtones in this play. That Alvaro's daughter becomes just like her father is very painful.[26] She, too, refuses the world before the conclusion of the play and also plans to spend her life in contemplation of God.

*Le Maître de Santiago* hardly seems to be tragedy because there is no basic conflict in the play and the leading character, Alvaro, learns nothing in the course of the action, and the play concludes, therefore, as pessimistically as it began. He has refused life when the play opens and retains that attitude throughout the drama. Nothing can dissuade him from his exile, not even the consideration of the happiness of his daughter. The play becomes, therefore, a study of character, a study of a man of superior qualities who has refused to live in his century. As such it is an important document in the modern dramatic literature of exile. As a tragedy, however, it is a failure.

If Alvaro lives in solitude because he chooses to do so, Malatesta is a solitary man who lives in the turmoil of the world and participates in it. Yet he, too, lives in a state of spiritual exile from his century. He is, however, not the only man in *Malatesta* who lives in loneliness. The majority of the characters do, but since he is the hero of the play it is his problems which are important to us.

Malatesta is not an exile, as Alvaro is, through religious faith and disgust with man. He is alienated because he is a superior man who is misunderstood by his contemporaries. The contradictions of his own personality give justification to this misunderstanding and his very superiority in martial affairs makes him an object of envy and hatred. His own character causes him to be the dupe of everyone who comes near him. He can be taken in by anyone who flatters him or even by anyone who speaks with an air of sincerity. Because of this he is poisoned by Porcellio, a man of letters at his court.

His alienation is well explained by his friend, Platina:

That you, the conqueror, and I, the scholar, that you and I, who by good and by evil are henceforth through the centuries part of the patrimony of Italy, should be treated as enemies of our country, and almost as common bandits, isn't something to moan over but rather something to be smiled at. Misfortune adds to our glory exactly as success does; and the two, moreover, taste exactly the same.[27]

Unappreciated by his country and betrayed by his friends, he is brought to Rome where the Pope imprisons him. The Pope tells him that he has served exclusively his own interests in life, that he is a monster. (The monstrous aspects of the personality of Malatesta resemble in some respects the monstrosity of Ferrante in killing Inès, of Alvaro in refusing happiness to his daughter, of Georges Carrion in his attitude towards his son, of the Abbé de Pradts in his breaking the friendship of the two young boys.) The strain of perversity and cruelty which runs through Montherlant's theatre is especially notable in Malatesta. The Pope lists Malatesta's crimes:

You make fun of Christianity. You make fun of Italy. Your family, your friends? You betrayed and tried to poison Sforza, your father-in-law. You are presumed to have strangled your first two wives. You tortured and killed your old tutor Ugolino de Pili. Nature? You slept with your son-in-law Camerino when he was an adolescent. You soiled with your lust the corpse of the beautiful German girl from Fano after having put her to death. . . .
Worse still—and I mention this crime only with a shiver of horror; you tried to possess your son Roberto, who had to seize a dagger to defend himself against you. . . .[28]

Malatesta, although he knows that much of what the Pope has said is true, claims that everyone believes him to be capable of everything, and in his ensuing speech describes his great solitude:

I am accused of what I have done, of what I have not done, and also of the same acts for which others are not blamed, when it is they who do them, and for which they are even praised. I am accused of everything I am believed capable of, and I am believed capable of everything because my enemies have gotten the upper hand in the fabrication of my legend; to justify oneself by public opinion, when one has himself created that opinion by repeated lying, is too easy. I am surrounded by hatred, a hatred which for thirty-five years has not disarmed. . . . And victory itself I have given, many times, to those who had entrusted me with their lives; I gave it to them in spite of them, against them, duped by them, betrayed by them, betrayed by my masters, betrayed by my brother, betrayed by my sons.

Hatred! Always hatred! Ah, how vile they will have been to me![29]

The pope understands Malatesta's predicament only too well, for he, being a man of power too, realizes the loneliness of the superior man. When Malatesta asks him why he should do good if no one will recognize it, he unconsciously foreshadows the ironic yielding of the Pope to the entreaties of Isotta, Malatesta's wife, to free him. The Pope has performed a good act but men will not see it as such; he says:

Perugia, I have just performed a good action. . . . She will always believe that I acted through calculation, that it was a trap. . . . My hand was raised; I did not strike him down; where will I receive credit for that? There ought, however, to be a reward when one performs a good action, if not a reward from others, at least a reward from oneself. But nothing, my God! No, nothing, my God! No, nothing, my God, for goodness. Or rather, yes, a punishment.[30]

One of Malatesta's chief delights is reading the ancient authors. In them he finds consolation for his solitude. History proves, he claims, that all illustrious men were in disgrace, condemned by their times.[31] But if Malatesta is interested in the classic authors, he is more interested in his own biography, because through it he hopes to be known to future ages. This biography is his *raison d'être*, and into it he puts the best and worst of himself. The irony of the fact that while he is dying his biography is burned by Porcellio is well underlined by Montherlant, because Malatesta's life, as he has seen it, his justification of himself, burns slowly as the poison takes effect in his system. They disappear together, and Malatesta dies in utter solitude. Jacques de LaPrade comments on Malatesta's final isolation when he says: "Be our battlefield a cell or the world, we never have any witnesses and our noise dies away."[32]

Porcellio has murdered Malatesta from jealousy but also from fear. He has seen Malatesta with his soul bare just as Inès had seen Ferrante, and, knowing that he might lose his life because of this, decides to act first. Malatesta has already told him: "That means that one must never touch a soul when it is uncovered and defenseless. How vulnerable one is in those moments."[33]

In *Malatesta*, Montherlant has painted the solitude of a man in whom there is a confusion and profusion of passions, a man to whom glory means everything. But his loneliness is painful, perhaps even more so than that of Alvaro who has retired from life, in whom the passions have given way to an austerity of spirit, to whom glory means nothing. Each man refuses his world, perhaps mainly because his world has no place for him. Each is too egotistical to give others credit for their virtues and therefore none can live up to his exigent standards. Ernest Bendz sums up the problems of the heroes of Montherlant when he speaks of their despair and pessimism, ". . . the despair of man before the lack of moral fiber in the individual and in the agglomeration of individuals beside whom he lives, and the despair of man before man's fate."[34]

Yet the exile of these men, like that of Ferrante, is essentially the solitude of superiority, of their aristocracy of mind as well as birth. Pierre Jaccard, speaking of Ferrante, although he might be speaking of all the Montherlant heroes, claims that Ferrante's solitude is that of his creator, also a superior man and an aristocrat:

In this play one sees transposed, on the level of artistic creation, the profound drama of the solitude of Montherlant. The character King Ferrante, in whom one finds some of the dominant character traits of our author, is really the poignant image of the solitary writer, feared by all, misunderstood by most, rejected by his own and before long banished under the cloud of injurious accusations. This time of war and defeat for France will have been for Montherlant what the hour of his last interview with Inès de Castro was for old King Ferrante.[35]

Montherlant, himself, reinforces this statement of Jaccard in passages in two of his essays. He writes:

Before 1925 I had courted notoriety. Now I lived in that sort of exile which one calls the disinterested life.[36]

The king, whose character is scarcely sketched in Guevera, was taking form, moulded with some of my characteristics. Each one of these creatures became in its turn the spokesman for one of my personalities . . . in short, *La Reine Morte* was falling into the rule which governs all my works, to which I apply the statement of Goethe about his: that they are never, one or another, anything but fragments from his memoirs.[37]

In speaking of himself in the first of these quotations, Montherlant proves himself, in many ways, to be a twentieth-century Alvaro, but an Alvaro without the consolation of complete communication with the Deity. In the second quotation we see not only how Ferrante was modeled after Montherlant but how Montherlant suggests that all his characters were taken from his own life and personality. Thus, in treating the aristocrat of former times, Montherlant is indicating most strongly the exile of the same type of person, notably himself, in the twentieth century. This procedure is exactly the same as that of many of the dramatic authors of the nineteenth century who, like Montherlant and in a way which we today should call romantic, expressed their own exile and that of the contemporary creative and superior person, by taking historical personages and endowing them with their own problems. The difference between Byron's *Cain* or Shelley's *The Cenci* and Montherlant's *Malatesta* is basically only one of style. Montherlant, who was born one hundred years later than Byron and Shelley, could easily be their spiritual brother.

Thus, we may say that in the modern theatre there are three distinct types of aristocratic exiles, all of them lonely people. The Chantemelles have been rejected by their age and are decaying in solitude. They are too proud to accept the modern world. Blanche and the early heroines of Tennessee Williams are rejected by their society because they cannot adjust even though they occasionally make a half-hearted effort to do so. The heroes of Montherlant are too proud of their own superiority even to think of adjusting. They merely turn their backs on a world which they do not respect. They are proud of their difference from other men and, unlike the Chantemelles and Blanche, seldom, if ever, complain of it. Of these three types, the decaying and isolated aristocrat, the aristocrat in contact with the modern world, and the aristocrat with superior endowments, the last has the most pessimistic connotations. In Montherlant's theatre there seems to be no remedy for the exile of the superior man. Time and again the reader is told that superior men throughout history have been exiled from their ages. Yet if his aristocratic heroes are supposed to be tragic, Montherlant fails. Because of their colossal egos we do not feel sorry for them. They have chosen their exile and are contented with it. Their attitude, like that of all the Chantemelles except Robert, is essentially negative, for through their pessimistic views they ultimately deny the value of life. They condemn their contemporaries but do not justify themselves or man. Much more pathetic are Blanche and Robert, who at least see their predicament in human terms and who occasionally realize that each question has two sides.

## Chapter III

# The Lower Depths

THE drama of the nineteenth century was as concerned with man's soul as is its twentieth-century counterpart. In the Romantic drama the struggles in man's soul are present, but there is little analysis of these struggles and we are often unaware of the reasons for their existence. The *mal du siècle* of Antony, Hernani, Ruy Blas, and Chatterton has a complementary element of mystery; we know these characters suffer, but we do not always know why. We see the effects of their suffering—their alienation from society—but there is little diagnosis of the ill itself. It is, perhaps, for this reason that the Romantic hero of the last century has more the attributes of a *papier mâché* figure than those of a convincing dramatic creation. His portrayal is almost always exterior.

Conversely, the heroes of many of our contemporary dramatists fail to come to life because the portrayal of them is almost exclusively interior. The often obscure anti-social desires and impulses of the nineteenth-century hero which make of him a social outcast have been diagnosed, explicated, and dissected in his twentieth-century counterpart. The spiritual and moral differences between the modern heroes and other men are so strikingly demonstrated that these heroes have too often become merely case histories of psychological, pathological, and spiritual diseases. The attempts at analysis of Lenormand and Bourdet, and to a lesser extent of Martin du Gard and Julien Green, have led these authors to difficulties which did not plague the dramatists of the nineteenth century. Yet the heroes of both centuries are similar in many respects. They are out of joint with their times; they suffer from an interior malady; they hate the society which nurtured them.

But the Romantic playwrights cast over their heroes an aura of poetry which somehow lessens the horror of the usually unexplained torments of their heroes. Their art, being poetic basically, is one of suggestion rather than one of analysis. The poetry has disappeared in the plays of Lenormand, Bourdet, Green, and Martin du Gard. Analysis has triumphed, but when the analysis is finished and the characters stand bare before us, we are not certain that the detailed dissection has created characters any more believable than those created by the Romantics. We know more about the modern characters in these plays of psychological analysis because the night side of their life has reached the surface momentarily and then once more subsided to the lower depths; but whereas it is easy for us to understand them and their problems, these characters seldom remain engraved in our memories once they have left the stage, except perhaps as curiosities. Their curse is not the curse of a blind fate wreaking havoc on all-too-susceptible men, but rather that of desire which is too suffused for them to be able to cope with it. Like their Romantic predecessors, these heroes have been cast aside by society, but they are not portrayed, as their predecessors were, as being better than that society.

In our plays of psychological analysis, and especially in those of Lenormand, one is not altogether sure whether society was not right in casting them aside. Gone are the noble qualities Dumas, Vigny, and Hugo tell us that their characters possess. Instead, in our plays of the lower depths, we see little men and women grovelling before the picture they have painted of themselves as misfits, a picture which they almost masochistically enjoy but which terrifies them and makes them will-less at the same time. The ultimate failure of the plays of the lower depths derives from the fact that the heroes in them are too inhuman and conscienceless to be at all indicative, except to the most morbid and perverse pessimist, of man's fate. They are too bizarre to be universal.

The publication of the works of Sigmund Freud in the late nineteenth century had much influence on the analytical technique in the theatre and, consequently, on the study of the subconscious of man. What the Romantic playwrights did not dare to say about their characters—that Manfred was a repressed homosexual, Chatterton a manic-depressive, Antony a victim of dementia praecox—the modern playwright has been able to say of his because of the effects of the Freudian revolution on the temper of the times. The portrayal of homo-

sexuality in the contemporary theatre would have been un-
thinkable had it not been for this change in the mentality of
the public, and it is in the portrayal of homosexuality in the
modern theatre that the effects of the Freudian revolution are
best seen.

Previously homosexuality had been treated seldom, if ever,
by a French playwright. It was a subject which would not
have been permitted in the court dramas of the seventeenth
or eighteenth centuries because good taste forbade it. It was
too shocking a subject for the nineteenth-century theatre; a
theatre which aroused protests when a courtesan was depicted
on the stage[1] would never have tolerated a homosexual.[2] In
fact, little of the world's dramatic literature contains plays in
which the homosexual has been a major protagonist. There
were scenes in the Greek theatre which portrayed homosexual love;[3] for example, one of the lost plays of Sophocles
is said by Gilbert Norwood[4] to deal with the love of Achilles
for Patroclus.[5] But if the Greeks were moved and exalted by a
love scene between two men, few, if any, succeeding cultures
were moved in the same manner.

Homosexuality never again achieved the privileged and
often exalted place it held among the Greeks. It existed in
Rome. It existed in the Middle Ages: witness the charges
made against the Knights Templar in the fourteenth century.[6]
Indeed, though it has existed in all countries and in all ages, it
has survived only underground since the fall of Rome. Western
Europe has feared, hated, and persecuted the homosexual.
Even in its most enlightened periods it has held him in dis-
repute. In the Renaissance, when Platonic friendships between
men were a fashion and often prized highly, the obtrusive
homosexual was treated as a criminal. A genius like Leonardo
da Vinci could be, and was, accused of indulging in homosexual practices; in his youth he was supposedly imprisoned for
them.[7] This attitude of hostility persisted in Europe into the
twentieth century.

The creative artist has avoided sympathetic treatment of
the homosexual unless he is actually an apologist for him. In
fact, after the Greeks there was little in European literature
until the early twentieth century that was at all concerned
with him.[8] To be sure, there are intimations in the *Mémoires*
of the Cardinal de Retz of the homosexual practices of his
day. In Rousseau's *Confessions*[9] and in Voltaire's *Dictionnaire*

*philosophique*[10] there are passages in which homosexuality is mentioned, although seldom at length, and it is always condemned. Even in Balzac's *La Fille aux yeux d'or* the subject is mentioned as briefly as possible.[11] It seems almost as if the authors of the eighteenth and nineteenth centuries felt an obligation not to remind their public that sexual deviants existed.

If homosexuality was ignored or barely hinted at in previous centuries, the twentieth century has more than compensated for the long silence. Beginning with Gide and Proust, deviants themselves, who portrayed the homosexual in all his complexity and with the many artistic resources they had at hand, major writers began discussing and portraying homosexuality.[12] A change had occurred in the mentality of the public, and the literary artists took advantage of this change.

The change had been subtly appearing since the nineteenth century. The Romantic movement, with its emphasis on eccentricity, individuality, and abnormality, sufficiently shocked a public lost in the precarious self-assurance of neo-classicism and made men aware of their differences as well as of their similarities. The morality of the Victorians and their French counterparts under the Second Empire, who were on the surface proper and restrained, only partially covered the sexual and intellectual ferment beneath the existing social structure. The arrival of the pure art movements in the last half of the nineteenth century re-emphasized the rebellion of the romantic artist and his absolute insistence upon freedom from restraint. With the appearance of Freud late in the nineteenth century these movements came to psychological fruition. Because of and concurrent with Freud there appeared to be an increased interest in man's sexual mores on the part of the intelligent segments of the public, and the homosexual became a subject for study and understanding. But if society is more liberal now in its acceptance of him as a person, it still regards him as apart from the social group. Because he may be an extremely valuable member of society, the hostile attitude of his fellows tends to give him his tragic justification. His abnormality is his flaw, and it usually brings about his downfall.

The effects of the change in public thinking are apparent in the literature written since 1920. In the two decades following the First World War author after author began to portray or discuss the homosexual. A great many of these authors, taking advantage of the public interest in sexual deviants, wrote sensational literature,[13] but others used the homosexual as an artistic resource rather than as a financial expediency. In his provocative study of American novelists since the Second World War, *After the Lost Generation*, John Aldridge finds that one of the recurrent themes in the contemporary novel is homosexuality. He says:

One explanation is, as I have already shown, that the homosexual is one of the last remaining tragic types. His dilemma, like that of the Negro and the Jew, provides a conflict which is essentially presentable in fiction and which can be made to symbolize the larger conflicts of modern man.[14]

Henri Peyre, in a recent book on the modern French novel, also finds homosexuality to be one of the recurrent themes in the works he studies.[15] Homosexuality is found in the novels of Gide, Proust, Larbaud, Martin du Gard, Montherlant, Morand, Green, Sartre, and Peyrefitte, and it is certainly a recurrent theme in the works of Cocteau and Genêt.

The treatment of homosexuality in the novel was bound to influence the theatre eventually. But the theatre, which depends more than the novel upon immediate audience response, could not present homosexual characters until the psychologists and novelists had made the minds of men more receptive to considerations of the problems of the sexual deviant.

In the twenty years following the First World War France's theatre-going public saw four significant plays produced which dealt almost exclusively with homosexuality.[16] Disclaiming Freud's influence, Lenormand wrote *L'Homme et ses fantômes*, a psychological study of a contemporary Don Juan whose numerous and very temporary love affairs with women serve only to compensate for his real though unconscious love for his male friend. In 1926 Bourdet wrote *La Prisonnière*, a play portraying a Lesbian and the repercussions of her secret anomaly on her family. This play enjoyed a *succès de scandale* in Europe as well as in the United States, where it was eventually banned by the censors. Bourdet also wrote several years later another play—*La Fleur des pois*—which dealt with homosexuality; this time, however, he treated inversion as comedy. *La Fleur des pois* is a brilliant, if innocuous, satire on the mores of the degenerate aristocracy and café society of Paris in the early thirties. The finest play about homosexuality in these two decades is Roger Martin du Gard's *Un Taciturne,* a powerful and moving study of a man whose homosexual tendencies become apparent when he is middle-aged, and whose discovery of them causes him to commit suicide.

Homosexuality continued to be an important theme in the drama of the 1940's and 1950's. In Sartre's *Huis-Clos* a Lesbian is one of the three main characters, and she is the most sympathetically treated at that. Montherlant's *La Ville dont le prince est un enfant* is about a priest in a Catholic school who is unaware of, yet prey to, his homosexual tendencies. Perhaps the finest of the homosexual plays since the Second World War is Julien Green's *Sud,* first produced in 1953. This play presented in a delicate and profoundly nuanced, albeit naturalistic style, the character of a young Pole, Ian Wicziewsky, who, while serving in the American Army of the Republic, falls in love with a young Southerner who does not return his love. The Pole commits suicide by not defending himself in a duel with the young man. In recent years other plays such as Roussin's *Les Oeufs de l'autruche,* a comic trifle about an effeminate lad, and Genêt's basically vulgar drama about criminal homosexuals have appeared, but, Sartre not withstanding, these attempts do not seem destined to last as significant drama.

The author of *La Prisonnière,* the most famous of the homosexual plays of this century, is an intellectual, although, fortunately, not an artistic descendant of Eugène Brieux and the social playwrights of the turn of the century. The plays of Bourdet are not *pièces à thèse,* but like those of Brieux they are concerned mainly with social problems. Bourdet treats these problems on a less broad scale than Brieux although the latter's attitude of social pity is found echoed in Bourdet's *La Prisonnière* where, because of the author's attitude of pity towards his heroine, the tragic emphasis is misplaced, making the play less effective than it otherwise might have been.

Bourdet has most of the good qualities of Brieux, including a social conscience (in the constructive sense of the term), and few of the bad ones. He, too, occasionally seems to write with a view to social reform, but he is primarily a comic satirist. When his bitterness does not overwhelm him, as it does in *Les Temps difficiles,* his plays can be extremely effective because they are well constructed and the dialogue is always brittle, if not brilliant.

Irène, the heroine of *La Prisonnière*, although not a tragic figure, is as close to a tragic heroine as Bourdet comes in his plays. A Lesbian, she is a woman whose apparent helplessness coupled with an utter disregard of others effectively lessens any sympathy one might have for her. She is a completely passive person who acts only through fear of accepting a reality—her Lesbianism—and this passivity causes her to vacillate between her lover, Mme d'Aiguines, and her husband, Jacques.[17] When she is with Jacques she has some security; at least he will help her if she refuses to help herself, and she takes pride, when he essays to master her emotions, in what is only a temporary victory for him. She is really safe, however, only so long as she is not confronted with desire. The moment temptation appears in the person of Mme d'Aiguines Irène loses her equilibrium and succumbs to her Lesbian tendencies.

Irène is always desperate because she recognizes and yet will not completely accept her aberration. Trusting no one, and least of all herself, she continually stretches out her arms to the nearest person who might help her. This person is usually Jacques, but she takes advantage of his love for her only halfheartedly, instead of clinging to it with all her strength in order to be saved.[18] She appears to be a weak person who does not know her own mind or who will not accept its dictates; she will not meet reality on its own terms.

Jacques, who had hopes of redeeming her, exhausts his patience, and when she asks him for the last time to remove her from temptation by taking her away from Paris he refuses:

You want to know why? Look at yourself! Look at your face! That eager sensual look, those rolling eyes, those trembling hands. And all because you've seen her again. That's why! . . . For a year I have lived with a statue and that woman had only to reappear for the statue to come to life, to become a living person capable of suffering and becoming ecstatic! Well, I give up, Irène. Do you understand? I give up.[19]

Irène has only one recourse—to accept her anomaly. The symbol of her capitulation is a bouquet of violets sent by Mme d'Aiguines. Irène has carried them in the first act, and she receives them at the end of the play. The stage directions are instructive here:

The maid leaves. Irène continues to fix the violets. Slowly her eyes fill with tears. She raises the bouquet to her face, touches it lightly with her lips, and puts it against her cheek. Her eyes, becoming hard, turn for an instant towards the door through which Jacques has left, then return to the flowers and contemplate them for a long time. Finally, incapable of resisting any longer the call emanating from them, she gets up, goes to the door on the left, turns around one last time, as if she were still hesitant, and then goes out quickly.[20]

Temptation has grown too strong to be denied. Irène has accepted her Lesbianism.

The role of the Lesbian (and, by inference, of the male homosexual, too) is discussed by the most pathetic character in the play, M. d'Aiguines, whose misfortune it is to be married to, and still in love with, a Lesbian. He explains to Jacques that Lesbians must be avoided; once they enter the realms of Lesbianism they never return:

They are ghosts, and they must be left to walk with their kind in their ghostly kingdom. Don't approach! They are dangerous. Above all don't try to do anything for them, as little as it might be. That's the danger, for they still have some need of us. It's not always easy for a woman to make a living. So, if a man proposes to help her, to share his wealth with her, and give her his name, she accepts, naturally. What harm can that do her? Provided she's not asked to make love, she's not miserly about the rest. But imagine what the existence of that man must be if he has the misfortune to love, to adore the ghost with whom he lives. Can you imagine it? . . . Well, old boy, believe me, it's a beastly life! One gets worn out quickly in that sort of business. One gets old before his time, and, at thirty-five, look, one has gray hair. There you are![21]

He continues in an impassioned speech, the most powerful and touching bit of writing in the play, to paint the destruction a Lesbian can cause when she enters a man's home and seduces his wife:

It's mysterious . . . and dreadful. Friendship. Yes, that's the mask. Under cover of friendship a woman comes into a home whenever she wishes, as she wishes, at any time of the day, and she poisons everything in it. She ransacks everything in it, without the man, whose home is being destroyed, even noticing what is happening to it. When he becomes aware of it, it is too late. He is alone. Alone before the secret alliance of two beings who understand each other, who guess each other's thoughts because they are alike, because they are of the same sex, of another world than he, the stranger, the enemy. There you are! Ah, against a man

who wants to take your wife you can defend yourself; you at
least fight with the same weapons and you can always knock
his head off. But with them . . . there is nothing you can
do . . . except leave, when you can, when you have the
strength. And that's what you must do.[22]

When Jacques tells Irène that she is a statue, he is unknowingly criticizing her as an artistic creation. She is not a tragic
figure in any sense (she might have been) and she is seldom
likable. She is, as Jacques says, only a statue. Forces act about
her continually, but she remains almost completely passive.
Occasionally her monochromatic character takes on a little
coloring as in her brief scene with her sister, Gisèle, where she
evinces some tenderness for the young girl, and twice in scenes
with Jacques, although even then for only a few brief moments. In one of these scenes she tries to explain her anomaly
to him:

Irène:     You don't understand that there are moments as right
           now when I see clearly, when I have my wits about
           me, when I have free will. . . . But at other times I
           don't have it any more. I no longer know what I'm
           doing. It's like . . . a prison to which I have to re-
           turn in spite of myself! I am. . . .
Jacques:   Fascinated. . . .
Irène:     Yes. . . . Someone would have to guard me, hold me
           back. . . . Someone who might have understood or
           guessed certain things . . . that I can't tell, that I will
           never tell![23]

Irène is more of a woman than a statue here. The only other
time her character comes alive is in the third act when her
bluff has been called and her fury has gotten the better of her:

Irène:     I have done everything I could to love you! . . . You
           always speak of what you have done. And I? Have
           you ever known anything about my disgust? Have
           you ever been concerned with that? . . . You loved me,
           yes, but in your own way.[24]

One is left, at the end of the play, however, with the feeling
that Irène will become a real character of flesh and blood
once she returns to Gomorrah, but that, of course, does not
make her a more effective stage personage. Her portrayal as
a Lesbian might even have been avoided. As Gide remarks in
his *Journal*:

However clever Bourdet's play may be, and perhaps because of its very cleverness, I am embarrassed by a sort of indirect flattery of the public's worst instincts. It seems here that the highest felicity can be achieved only in coitus. . . . I understand only too well the distress of Bourdet's hero when faced with the painful evidence of his inability to give his wife more joy, and his wife's inability to experience a sincere and complete joy with him. But that hero, whom he depicts at the outset as so noble, descends to the point of degradation when he bases his happiness on *that* . . . it would seem according to Bourdet, that heterosexuality is enough to ensure happiness. The drama, after all, might be the same without his heroine's being "a captive"; I am not even sure that it might not have been better.[25]

La Prisonnière is basically a social drama rather than a tragedy; it is the painting of an anomaly and the effect of that anomaly on a family. As such, it is reminiscent of Brieux's Les Avariés, which is concerned with syphilis as a social problem. In the former play, however, the significance of the Lesbian in the modern world is shown only in the limited circle of the ménage whereas in Les Avariés the problem of syphilis extends not only to the larger family but to all society.

If in La Prisonnière Bourdet presented a social tableau over which he has diffused some delicate pastel shadings which neither obscure nor clarify to any great extent any segment of the picture (thus painting a social situation whose colors are too diffuse to have any profound meaning), Roger Martin du Gard has in Un Taciturne painted a picture which is sharply focused upon one man, and the resulting centralization gives power and meaning to his creation.

Thierry of Un Taciturne is a homosexual who is unaware of his own propensities. He is a more appealing and more pathetic character than Irène, for he at least battles throughout the play against an unknown—his homosexuality—which is revealed to him only in the last act. The shock of realizing his aberration comes upon him so suddenly that, despairing, he sees the futility of his love for a young man, realizes he has transgressed, and commits suicide.[26]

Unlike Irène, who is a weak person, eventually resigning herself to her status of Lesbian, Thierry is a strong person who does not vacillate. He struggles against something he does not, cannot, and will not understand. To him, homosexuality is abominable, its adherents victims of a hopeless perversion. He is ashamed when he recognizes his own tendencies and prefers death to breaking a moral code he has long upheld. He is presented as a proud, solid, commanding man, a man who knows what he wants and who is assured of getting it. His self-assurance, together with his inability to tolerate deviation from the moral code, will contribute eventually to the *dénouement*.

Thierry is seen differently by the other major characters in the play. His sister, Isabelle, sees him as solid, strong, domineering.[27] To be useful to him, she finds that "one must be his slave; a person who had no pliability of character, no submissiveness, would be useless to him."[28] Thierry's cousin, Armand, sees him as a bear who should be left alone, and tells him, "You always seem so out of place in this world."[29] Wanda, whom Thierry claims he once loved and who is a close friend staying with Thierry's family, finds him repugnant; she could not go to bed with him.[30] None of these characters suspects Thierry's latent homosexuality, however, until later in the play. He causes them all some uneasiness, but none knows exactly why until, with the audience, they begin to glimpse the reason as his homosexual tendencies appear.

The first hint of his aberration appears when Joë applies for a non-existent job and is given it.[31] Joë is a charming young man, "a little rooster," as Wanda describes him.[32] He would capture anyone's sympathies and, with his appearance at the end of the first act, which has started slowly, the pace of the play increases and never slows down thereafter. In the second act we first suspect Thierry's weakness, as he watches Joë exercising in a bathing suit. His interest in the young man, coupled with a slight jealousy of Wanda,[33] begins the more and more obvious external manifestations of Thierry's love. Wanda notices Thierry's attitude and suggests that he might be taken in by the youth. Thierry categorically denies this, but misses the point of Wanda's remark and turns immediately, perhaps as a reflexive cover-up, to a discussion of his relations with women.[34] He tells Wanda how he loved her:[35]

And yet I loved you, Wanda . . . loved you! . . . I loved you! With a tender, very special love . . . almost chaste! That's true! I loved you so much that I almost didn't desire you! . . . But you repulsed me. . . .[36]

Thierry then tells her that he has had women but that never did a woman love him. He cannot understand this fact. Wanda

sees through his rationalizations and makes him uneasy by
appearing to know something he does not. She tries to comfort him:

But, my friend, perhaps it is not so much being loved that matters. . . . But what would be sadder and more serious would be
never having been able to love.[37]

This statement is ambiguous. It could refer to Thierry and
his previous women, or to Thierry and Joë, or to Wanda's own
feelings for Isabelle. In any case it does not give Thierry
much comfort.

By the time the second act has finished, not only Wanda
but Armand has guessed the truth about Thierry's interest in
Joë. The third act is the culmination of the tragedy, and
everybody is prepared for it but Thierry. The astonishing
manner in which Martin du Gard has developed his hero's
final conscious realization of his love for Joë is masterly.
When Isabelle tells her brother that she is going to marry
Joë, her words bring to the fore Thierry's subconscious
jealousy of her. He tries unsuccessfully to subdue his emotions, and his attempts to dissuade Isabelle from marriage are
those of a jealous suitor. But, failing to move Isabelle, he tries
to dissuade Joë from the marriage by playing on the youth's
egotism and sense of independence. His words sound strangely
like those d'Aiguines uses in his speech to Jacques in *La
Prisonnière*:

It's marriage which is terrible. . . . To let yourself be bound
hand and foot for your whole life to a person with a different
temperament, a different education, a different background. . . .[38]

Joë, unaware of his employer's love, answers Thierry's
next observation—that Joë is one of the supermen and must
remain free to accomplish his destiny—with a telling remark.
"You don't think that bachelors are the only ones who succeed in life!"[39] Joë then informs Thierry that he loves Isabelle, has had sexual relations with her, and will marry her.
Thierry becomes enraged, and his kindness toward Joë turns
to abuse and brutality.

Having failed to dissuade either Isabelle or Joë, and
realizing his helplessness, Thierry listens to Armand, who
essays to comfort him; but he misunderstands Armand's words,
which hint at the nature of Thierry's passion. Thierry believes he is speaking of incest with Isabelle.

Thierry: Do you think that if I had been . . . capable of . . . of
a feeling . . . so abominable . . . of such an aberration. . . .

Armand: "Aberration"! Naturally! Old boy, you can very easily
carry in yourself for years feelings that you don't even
suspect, and on which, moreover, you live! . . . And,
too, it's easy to say that you will fight them, but there
are things against which your will power is helpless.[40]

When Thierry realizes that Armand means that he, Thierry,
is in love with Joë, he is overwhelmed. He knows himself at
last, and he is ashamed.

Thierry: Don't look at me like that! . . . Don't speak! (*In a low
voice*) I am ashamed of myself. . . .

Armand: Shame? What has that got to do with it? As if each
person's temperament didn't have its quirks where physical love is concerned. . . . Are you going to establish
hierarchies and decree that this love is noble, that
that one. . . .[41]

Armand, the *raisonneur* of the play,[42] says that Thierry is more
concerned with the hopelessness of his love for Joë than his
homosexuality itself.[43] But his reasoning falls on deaf ears, and
Thierry, overwhelmed by the discovery of his nature, commits suicide.

Thierry is an exile not because society refuses to accept
his homosexuality, but rather because he is too proud to
permit society to accept it. His death therefore has meaning,
although the meaning is erroneous, because Thierry has enough
faith in man's laws and conventions, imperfect as they are,
to commit suicide rather than break them. Once his self-
assurance is destroyed his whole being is destroyed with it.
Irène accepted her Lesbianism because she could do little
else. It was a refuge, and she had a lover, Mme d'Aiguines,
who would protect her. Thierry has no protection, and he
feels that living in shame is worse than not living at all. His
sexual anomaly has set him apart from the society of which
he is a pillar, and because he is a pillar of that imperfect society he cannot live outside it; he has too much respect for
its laws.[44]

*Un Taciturne* has a broader significance than the story of
its hero: it is in many ways the condemnation of an epoch:

Armand: I am so very aware that it is impossible to ever change
anything.

Joë:      Do you know, Armand, that that's your own condemnation that you're signing there. It is even the
condemnation of a whole era.[45]

That Thierry should be as he is, afraid either to be himself
or to recognize his own deviation, seems to Martin du Gard
symbolical of man in our times. The man whose deviation is
known is scorned, maltreated, persecuted. If he does not
conform to the norms of society he becomes alienated, and
Thierry recognizes this fact only too well.

What Martin du Gard is implying is that there is no
norm. Man is what he is, and with his bad qualities there are
undoubtedly good ones. Because one is neither black nor
white, but only a shade of grey somewhere in between, one
should accept one's own deviations and those of others as
well, as long as the deviations are from conventions and not
from laws.

Conformism, just for the sake of conforming, the author
says, often emphasizes unresolved psychological difficulties.[46]
Like half of a pair of scissors, man, emasculated by society,
has become impotent, powerless to carry through his contri-
butions to life in the manner in which they should be accomplished.[47] Man has lost his individuality and can no longer
freely express himself because of his fear of the opinions of
others. But, as in the case of Thierry, this repression of
natural instincts can lead only to breakdown and creative, if
not physical, death.

*Un Taciturne* is an admirably constructed play. There is
irony and a sense of fatality in the inexorable flow of the
action where event succeeds event until the final tragedy is
achieved. This movement is reminiscent of the finest Greek
drama. Just as Oedipus, unaware of his own past, tempts
fate by examining further into his own background and
eventually discovers that by seeking the murderer of Laius
he is seeking himself, so Thierry asks why his father committed suicide, why he himself has never been loved by a
woman. Like Oedipus, when he discovers himself he also
finds his fate and the tragedy is culminated. Too, as in the
Greek play, irony is employed by the author to such an
extent as to give the play much of its power and to help clarify
many of the aspects of Thierry's alienation.[48]

Perhaps the most ironic element in the play, and here
Martin du Gard employs tragic irony to its fullest, is the

fact that throughout Thierry damns people who are the victims
of sexual aberrations. He has his own moral standard, and to
him others are unworthy unless they live up to it. He refuses
to believe, for example, that his father was sensitive to the
attractions of a young girl.[49] He speaks of "the most elemen-
tary morality"[50] to which everyone should adhere or be
punished. It is not surprising therefore that Thierry, living in
a state of false security, should be overwhelmed when he discovers that he, too, is the victim of a sexual aberration.
Dramatic irony has run its course.

The parallels between the relationship Thierry-Joë and
the relationship Isabelle-Wanda are also ironic.[51] Wanda is
jealous of Isabelle as Thierry is of Joë. When Isabelle decides
to marry Joë, Wanda becomes furious, and when she discovers that Isabelle has had sexual relations with the young
man she is shattered. The stage directions read, "Sudden sobs
choke her."[52] She even goes to Thierry to try to have him
stop the marriage, but it is too late for him to do that, even
though he, too, rages when he hears of the marriage plans.
Although he does not want to lose Joë any more than Wanda
wants to lose Isabelle, he, as she, loses the object of his affections. Wanda does not commit suicide, however. She has been
aware of her own status and has accepted her deviation. In
comparison Thierry has been deluding himself and others, too.
He and Wanda pursue similar and parallel paths, but one is
aware of her direction; the other is not. The irony is that
Thierry dies while Wanda lives.

Irony plays a large part in making the audience aware that
Thierry is different from others. The audience must know of
his deviation before he does or else the shock will be too
great to be believed. As in *Oedipus Rex*, one of the functions
of the dramatic irony in this play is to prepare the audience for
the eventual climax.

Although the language of *Un Taciturne* is not poetic or
especially brilliant, it serves its function by underlining the
ironies of the play. The characters are masterfully drawn, and
the psychological development of the action is superbly
handled. There are few other writers in the contemporary
French theatre who employ irony as effectively as Martin du
Gard in *Un Taciturne*. There are few other plays which
approach the inexorable pace and whirlwind climax of Greek
tragedy. There are few others whose heroes evoke as much
sympathy as Thierry.

Gide gives us some interesting sidelights on the production of *Un Taciturne* which help to point up the fact that the audience as well as many of the actors and the author himself considered Thierry (and, by inference, the homosexual in general) to be an exile. In commenting on Jouvet's and Renoir's conception of the play Gide says:

The secret motive of the play, moreover, seems completely incomprehensible to Jouvet and to Renoir. Not the slightest tremor, not the slightest warmth. If sensuality does not enter in, the pistol-shot at the end has no justification. . . .[53]

But Jouvet and Renoir act for a living and therefore have to compromise with their public.

"Such things happen," Roger Martin du Gard makes Armand say in his play, "such things happen, even to the best people." For fear of protests, Jouvet successively dropped the "even to the best people," then the following day, "such things happen." Where will that get him? He has ceased to say it; but still "such things happen" just the same, and the indignation of the conformists can do nothing about it.[54]

Thierry comes closer to being a tragic figure than many of our other dramatis personae. And yet he, too, fails to become a great tragic figure. His death seems more an attack on the narrow viewpoint and general sickness of his contemporaries than a justification of existence. One has the impression at the conclusion of *Un Taciturne* that not only is society, as seen through Thierry's eyes and through his actions in the course of the play, sick, but that Thierry himself is being condemned too. Martin du Gard seems to say that society should change its attitude toward sexual deviations, and, at the same time, he questions whether it ever will.

Because Thierry puts too much faith in the dubious conventions of man his death seems meaningless. His suicide is a justification of the very thing his creator questions, the correctness of the outlook of society. The established social order triumphs in *Un Taciturne*, and the responsibility for this triumph lies with Thierry. His death is unnecessary, therefore, if he is to be someone whom we admire, because neither society nor the homosexual has been justified in the course of the play. Thierry has not proved, as Lear and Oedipus do, that man can triumph over himself and over other men, even in death; in short, that man can have occasional majesty.

Both *La Prisonnière* and *Un Taciturne* are social plays rather than tragedies—and their alienated protagonists are personifications of social problems. We learn much by inference about the society which has cast aside Irène and Thierry; we learn that difference and individuality, as Martin du Gard makes explicit, are scorned or trampled under the heel of a mediocre conformity, and that death without meaning and disintegration are its inevitable results. What distinguishes these plays, and especially *Un Taciturne*, from classic tragedy is that the established order—represented by Thierry, the Victorian moralizer as well as the criminal—is the villain here and that it wins. The result is pessimism, a note on which classic tragedies seldom conclude.

Although Lenormand was, perhaps, the most influential French dramatist of the nineteen-twenties, today the chief value of his works lies in their historical importance as period pieces which express the psychological interests of his contemporaries. The realm of mind which the author of *Le Simoun* explored had previously been charted by Freud, whose theories, as Lenormand avers in his *Confessions d'un auteur dramatique*, were unknown to him during the years in which he wrote his plays. This realm, the mystic half-world where the conscious and the sub-conscious meet and battle, where men differ most from one another, this realm of shadows, rather than the sphere of light where men are or pretend to be similar, had interested no major playwright in France since the time of Crébillon. In the thirty years since the plays of Lenormand were most popular this world has become commonplace, and the stage in western Europe and America has been peopled with so many psychotic heroes and heroines who have not been able to distinguish in any coherent manner between illusion and reality that many theorists of the modern drama have been forced to search for a new definition of the tragic hero that would replace the long-defended Aristotelian concept.

One element in the psychological constitution of many modern stage heroes which most of these theorists have overlooked or, at best, to which they have granted perfunctory attention is desire, especially physical desire and its relation to death, desire as an escape from reality, as a *modus vivendi*. In the works of playwrights as dissimilar as Sartre and Mauriac, Anouilh and Giraudoux, one finds extended treatment of characters whose motivating obsession appears to be desire, in the sense of physical lust, and whose only escape is death. Nowhere is this more apparent than in the works of H.-R. Lenormand.

The heroes of Lenormand are, in general, physically, spiritually, or morally decadent: cowards, robbers, psychotics, homosexuals, prostitutes, spies, deserters, fetishists, half-breeds, degenerates, and roués are his dramatis personae. These people are incapable of action because they live in a state of perpetual uncertainty about their own desires, desires which obsess them to such an extent that life becomes meaningless and is, in reality, nothing more than a living death. Aïescha, the half-breed mistress of Laurency in *Le Simoun* speaks of the Arabs as being a restless race and extends the classification to include the whole race of man. She explains unknowingly why each man in Lenormand's theatre is disintegrating, why he is unsatisfied and solitary:

He is poor, he is unhappy, and he desires . . . he desires eternally. When I say the Arab, I could just as well say the Black . . . or even the White . . . (*She laughs*) Man! Man! Man![55]

This passage provides us with an excellent insight into the meaning and significance of Lenormand's theatre. What does Aïescha mean when she says that man is poor? *Pauvre* here has the emphatic suggestion of poor meaning in want. In want of what? The answer is found in all of Lenormand's plays, but the Troll in *La Folle du ciel*, acting as a sort of *deus in machina*, best answers this question:

And man will see his instinct engulfed by intelligence. Master of heaven and earth, he will have, to protect his life, less wisdom than a slug or a crab. He will continue stupidly to play with the forces which destroy him.[56]

He is, therefore, in want of a sense of proportion and will play with natural forces which do not concern him until he is destroyed by them. Because man aims at the impossible and has neither the strength of character or body nor the will to achieve his ideals, he is destined to ruin. This is Lenormand's conception of his heroes, and one finds in this concept much that is related to the classic definition of a stage hero. But there are differences, differences which prohibit the characters of Lenormand from being tragic and his plays from being tragedies. His characters are *pauvre*, which classic heroes are not. These twentieth-century stage figures lack that sense of an ordered universe with inflexible laws, a world of which they are a part and in which they participate. The heroes of Lenormand are self-centered to the point of excluding the world from their ken, and they thus impoverish themselves and their world. They are forced to rely upon only their own idiosyncrasies in order to maintain even a semblance of humanity, and it is for this reason, among others, that Lenormand's plays ultimately fail.

The hero of Lenormand is *pauvre* in another sense too: he places no faith whatsoever in truth, his own reason, or his conscience. In play after play we are informed that conscience is the cholera of modern man,[57] that truth is a dog that should be muzzled,[58] that logic has no place in the contemporary world,[59] that art is an enemy of thought and conscience.[60]

If man, however, removes reason, abstract truth or ideals, and conscience from his life he becomes a prey to his emotions, and such happens not infrequently in the theatre of Lenormand. His heroes having removed, or trying to remove, reason from their existence, remove at the same time the major distinction between man and animal, and they become almost exclusively creatures of emotion and instinct. Like Phèdre they may say, "C'est Venus toute entière à sa proie attachée," but unlike her they are incapable of saying: "Il faut à votre fils rendre son innocence: Il n'était point coupable." Acting on instinct and emotion and striving toward uncertain goals, the only explicit one in Lenormand's theatre being self-knowledge which is never attained even when attempted, because of the distrust of the intellect, the heroes of the author of *Le Temps est un songe* are *malheureux*. They understand neither themselves as, say, a Phèdre or a Romeo does, nor their world as does an Oedipus. They battle constantly an unknown, which is usually the personification of their subconscious desires, and always lose because they fight without conviction. The secret of the hero of classical drama was his firm stand against his fate when it was made apparent to him, and in his struggle he gave meaning to life and dignity to man even though he was defeated. Lenormand's heroes, finding no meaning in life, struggle uselessly, and their inevitable defeat has no meaning.

Relying upon his instincts alone, the Lenormand hero

becomes the playmate of desire, and desire alone propels his life. L'Homme of *L'Homme et ses fantômes* says, "The man without desires would be a thinking corpse."[61] Without any sort of reason to guide him, the hero turns to an inner world peopled with monsters and memories of past holocausts, and spends much of his time recreating these events either verbally or in repeated obsessive actions. Thus Laurency in *Le Simoun* relives his passion for his wife by means of an incestuous mental relationship with his daughter, Clotilde. So Fearon and Rougé, having discovered the power of evil, recreate and carry through obsessive and deliberate acts of evil, helpless before their own desires. And Monique in *Mixture*, having experienced every form of degradation, tries to repeat her life by making her daughter relive the experiences she herself had undergone. We are far here from the noble savage of the eighteenth and nineteenth centuries. We are among savages in a savage world.

Love has no place in this world. The few characters in Lenormand's theatre who experience this emotion, such as Thérèse in *Une Vie secrète*, Aimée in *Asie*, Romée of *Le Temps est un songe* and La Mouette of *La Folle du ciel*, are weak and ineffectual characters whose existence is somehow dominated by people controlled by desire, men who scorn the word love because they are incapable of experiencing it.

What exactly then does desire mean in the theatre of Lenormand? The closest definition of it which we may find is that it is a way of living, *the* way of living, synonymous with the word life, because time and again it is suggested as being the opposite of death. The Prophet of *Le Simoun* says, "Then pray for eternal death which alone will appease desire."[62] Sarterre, the composer in *Une Vie secrète*, lives by desire which he, in his more lucid moments, does not consider a human sentiment. He claims that it leads only to self-destruction.[63] And so it does, because desire and death, like love and hate and other opposites, contain within themselves the seeds of each other. Desire, as Sarterre makes clear, is fleshly, not, he says, in a Gidean distinction, spiritual, because love is spiritual. Yet he prefers to live by desire because from it springs art, the creation of a world or, we might say, life.

The hero, however, who relies on desire because he is unhappy is made even more so because of this reliance. The

Prophet says, "You desire because you want to live and you suffer because you desire."[64] Upon hearing an Arab say that desire relieves the anguish of existence, the Prophet says:

Hypocrites! Don't tell me you are escaping pain! I know that at noon, behind your tabby walls, you lift your burnous and secretly show your ulcers.[65]

He continues:

But your hungers and thirsts will grow ceaselessly. . . . Your desires and your sores will grow more acute the closer you come to the grave. The young man booted in mud who seeks young girls with slender arms will seek them in his old age: he becomes the blackened vineshoot which writhes a long time in the flames without being able to burn away.[66]

Life, then, is synonymous with perpetual desire.

Desire to the characters of Lenormand is also a symbol of emptiness, of extinction, which once again shows its relation to death. Jeannine of *Le Mangeur de rêves* says to Luc de Brontë, "Your eyes burn all women, but you are an extinguished man . . . a cruel man, too."[67] The lovers of the Don Juan character in *L'Homme et ses fantômes* as well as Luc de Brontë, the *raisonneur* of the play, repeat the same thing to him. Lenormand's heroes are characters living a form of death. Their desire is not confined only to sexual matters, because tied up with these are various forms of ambition. The desire is never for one thing alone. Fearon says in *Mixture*, "If man were able to want only one thing he would be the master of the world."[68] But man in Lenormand's theatre wants everything and yet has not the strength or means to attain it. He therefore lives in a perpetual state of desire, and life for him becomes synonymous with this desire. Those who try to escape it are even more horrible examples of humanity. They flee into a state of absurdity. The Judge in *La Maison des remparts* plays with marionnettes. He says:

For an examining magistrate humanity has nothing very pleasant about it, you know. I think it's because of seeing alcoholic murderers, incestuous fathers, mothers who have committed infanticide, sadists and poisoners that I have developed a taste for these reductions of human misery and vice. And it's by contrast that the taste for innocent marionnettes with artless souls has come to me.[69]

The Vérificateur in *Le Simoun* repeats axioms to ward off desire, but his life, like the lives of those who embrace desire such as the Percepteur who must keep moving ever southward, the Receveur who spends his time chasing young girls, and Laurency who loves his daughter, is one of living death.

There is no escape from desire in the theatre of Lenormand, as there is none from *angoisse* in the theatre of Sartre. The Lenormand heroes find suicide the only answer. And this is the hallmark of Lenormand's theatre. Character after character commits suicide as the result of a strange exaltation experienced moments before, an exaltation in which life loses all meaning, and the idea of death as a release from desire becomes omnipotent.

We seldom find people of noble character in Lenormand's world, and when we do they are usually colorless people who serve merely as foils for the problems and perversions of the protagonists. The characters of Lenormand are passive people who live in a state of perpetual uncertainty. This state of passivity is induced by the sickness of personality of the leading characters. Climatic circumstances and personal solitude aggravate this condition, and interests in the supernatural and in magic represent attempts to avoid it, but these attempts are unsuccessful and the passivity of the hero leads to his defeat.[70]

The sicknesses of the characters are multiform. There are sexual sicknesses: homosexuality in *L'Homme et ses fantômes*, depraved eroticism in *Une Vie secrète*. There is moral sickness: cowardice in *Le Lâche*. There is spiritual sickness, a malady as a result of which the personality refuses to act and just stagnates, as in *Le Simoun*. There is the impotence of the creative personality: self-pity and lack of self-confidence in *Les Ratés*, *Crépuscule du théâtre* and *Les Trois Chambres*. There is the sickness of the split personality: the ambivalence without justification of a leading character's actions, as in *Mixture*, *Le Mangeur de rêves*, and *A l'Ombre du mal*. Each of these sicknesses is the cause of its possessor's alienation from society.

Each of Lenormand's plays contains at least one pathological character, usually the hero or heroine. Alongside these central characters are the minor ones who may be divided roughly into two groups. There are the normal ones, who are thoroughly uninteresting, such as Edouard in *L'Amour magicien*, Thérèse in *Une Vie secrète*, Aimée in *Asie*. And there are the characters whose sicknesses parallel those of the hero or heroine but in whom the results are different. This second group serves as ironic commentary on as well as contrast to the main characters. Such are La Vicelli in *Une Vie secrète*, Le Vérificateur in *Le Simoun*, Fearon in *Mixture* and *Le Mangeur de rêves*, Charlier in *Le Lâche*, Floret in *La Maison des remparts*.

The alienated heroes of Lenormand's theatre have many common traits.[71] Most of the characters in Lenormand's world seek fixity. They cannot find it because they do not understand their own instability or its origin. They tend to blame their uneasiness on others, unaware that they alone are responsible for it. The result, of course, is their complete unhappiness, their hypersensitivity, and their inability to adjust to the society in which they live.[72]

When Nico in *Le Temps est un songe* says, "We . . . that does not exist. . . . There is you. . . . There is I . . . I am alone,"[73] he is expressing another aspect of the Lenormand hero. Each of these heroes is lonely. He either seeks or lives in solitude, and, in seeking this solitude, he denies the world more often than not. Lui in *Les Ratés* tells Elle:

Then what's the use of wanting to become something? What's the difference between being honored or living in a molehill? Between being a genius or an old dotard? Since every man is condemned to the same imbecility? Rotting without having understood anything, without having achieved anything, as lonely and useless as carrion on the desert. . . .[74]

Pierre in *Les Trois Chambres* says:

Oh, our intimacy is so complete that it is equivalent to solitude. I long for solitude and I am not equal to it.[75]

In many respects Lenormand's theatre is reminiscent of the drama of Crébillon who also dealt with horror and hell, but the horrors of Crébillon's theatre become a sense of active evil in the plays of Lenormand. Time and again Lenormand's characters comment on evil, and in many cases it is this sense of evil which damns the various characters to exile. Fearon is an example of active evil. She tells Luc de Brontë, "Do you know what amuses me most in life? Seducing, corrupting a pure conscience. You, too, you like that."[76] Her actions bear out her words when she gives Jeannine a gun in the last act of *Le Mangeur de rêves*, knowing full well that Jeannine will kill herself with it.

Although most of Lenormand's characters are profoundly influenced by evil, and admit that it exists and is an extremely powerful force, none of them exploits it as much as Fearon or Rougé. John Palmer in his *Studies in the Contemporary Theatre* speaks of the role of evil in the plays:

The presence of a positive and active principal of evil is felt in every play of M. Lenormand, but there is one of them which is almost wholly concerned with the affirmation that evil exists, that it has its own logic and its own devotees, and that it is perpetually creative.[77]

This play, *A l'Ombre du mal*, has as leading character Rougé, who believes that the only justice is injustice, that evil is an end unto itself. Rougé is in the French administration in Equatorial Africa, but when he was younger he was the agent for a private company. One of his superiors ignored his requests for quinine and other necessities or else sent him the wrong materials. Two years of injustice and suffering instilled in Rougé a sadistic love of evil, and for the twenty years before the action of the play he has led a life of evil and injustice. To him, as to the other sick heroes of Lenormand, his malady is normal, the law of the universe.[78] He claims his acts were justified by the very fact of his being in Africa, and his relativism makes him exclaim that one can exist in this backward continent only through the practice of evil.[79] At the end of the play when Mme Le Cormier is murdered by the natives, one of whom Rougé has unjustly chastised, Rougé ironically exclaims that justice has been done.

Although Rougé is the chief exponent of the active force of evil in *A l'Ombre du mal*, other characters also realize its importance and live under its sway. Préfailles, who had formerly been Rougé's superior, has spent much of his life atoning for his cruelty to his subordinate. He sees the power of evil and recognizes it as something unavoidable: "Progress, goodness, even justice, for many of us, are fine memories, memories of Europe."[80] Even the young and idealistic Le Cormier recognizes the influence of evil by saying: "You women always seek reasons for wickedness. That's a roundabout way of justifying it. It doesn't need to be explained. It's natural."[81] Evil may be justice and the law of Africa but it has made of Rougé and Préfailles lonely people, exiles full of remorse, and yet who still believe in what has made them less than human.

In other of Lenormand's plays the characters are also aware of the power of evil. Lui in *Les Ratés* says that everything—power, possession, wealth—comes from evil. Sarterre asks Véra in *Une Vie secrète*, "What does being evil consist of?" She answers, "In avenging one's own suffering by wishing that of others."[82] The majority of Lenormand's heroes do just this. They make others suffer because they are incapable of suffering alone. It is a compulsion in the hero in each of the plays.

This sense of evil and the tendency to inflict one's personality and problems on, or see them in, others is a sign of alienation. The people who are affected by contact with these exiles usually see through them and tell them so, and this makes their solitude even more lonely and at the same time creates in the sick heroes a desire to inflict even more evil. And the cycle becomes endless.

Another quality which many of Lenormand's heroes have in common is an interest in the supernatural as a means of escaping the reality of this world. Nico has spent many years in the East and has been much influenced by oriental philosophy. But in his search for some sort of eternal truth he has become neurotic and desires only death. He is unable, as his oriental mentors are not, to contemplate and live at once, and when he discovers that the world is nothing but appearances and that eternal truth is beyond man's comprehension he takes his own life. Nico's interest in the supernatural is on a higher plane than that of other Lenormand heroes. The supernatural, however, plays a more important role in two other plays—*L'Homme et ses fantômes* and *L'Amour magicien*.

*L'Homme et ses fantômes* is the Don Juan story in modern dress. Lenormand has made of L'Homme (Don Juan) an unconscious homosexual whose numerous and very temporary affairs with women serve only to stress the fact that he is in love with his young friend, Patrice. Throughout the play we are aware, although he is not, of L'Homme's alienated status. He is, like Thierry of *Un Taciturne*, quite jealous of his young friend's affairs with women. He tells him several times, "But I don't think she's right for you. . ."[83] and, at one point, becomes furious when the young man sleeps with one of his own former mistresses. L'Homme does not understand, however, that he himself is homosexual. He wonders why he is unstable and lonely, why he feels so uncomfortable with women. His friend Luc de Brontë explains the reason:

The man who has possessed, then rejected dozens of women has suppressed woman from his life because he has suppressed love from it. He has continually protected himself, refused himself. He takes without giving. He believes he is chasing and he is fleeing. He doesn't seek to join forces but to conquer, to fight in retreat. He believes he wants joy; he only wants solitude. Sleeping with all women is equivalent to sleeping with none of them. Don Juan is a recluse. . . . In him the body is male and the soul female. . . . His body craves woman, his soul man. He seeks the ghost of man in woman. That's the reason that each of his victories is an intimate defeat.[84]

When this is revealed to him, L'Homme shuns Patrice and, because he has not accepted the explanation of Luc de Brontë and yet is still obsessed by his problem, turns to occultism. He attends seances at the establishment of a Medium. Luc de Brontë indicates that by so doing L'Homme has become exiled from everyday life; now that he has found the solitude he has been seeking he is peopling it with apparitions. L'-Homme craves solitude and yet cannot exist in such a state.

The section of the play concerned with the Medium symbolizes L'Homme's escape from the real world. Yet even his trips to the Medium become unbearable when the phantom of Alberte, a former mistress of his who has recently died, appears and tries to communicate with him. His only recourse is to remain within his own bedroom where he believes he will at least be safe. (Ironically the bedroom is the symbol of the place where he was least safe before.) But the world of apparitions does not disappear. It becomes too much with him and eventually replaces the exterior world. The play ends with L'Homme in his mother's arms trying to believe her when she tells him he is not really homosexual.

If the use of the supernatural is a means of representing the exile of L'Homme, it denotes even more clearly the alienation of Carolles in *L'Amour magicien*. In this odd and rather poor play, the spirit of Carolles' wife haunts the body of his secretary, Béatrice. Béatrice becomes subject to fits of fainting (or sleeping—one is never quite sure) and during these moments speaks with the voice of Berthe, Carolles' dead wife. Needless to say, Béatrice becomes obsessed with these spells and so does Carolles, who loses contact with reality as he digs further into the past to discover whether what the voice of Berthe says is true. Béatrice loves him, however, and Carolles asks her to marry him, believing that by so doing he can regain his peace of mind. However, the spirit of Berthe strangles Béatrice, and the play ends with Carolles in as much doubt as before and the reader unsure of the significance of the strangling.

Carolles is a writer who, while his wife was living, believed in the utility of his work. After her mysterious death he loses all interest in his creative ability because he has become too aware of himself. His sister, Fernande, says he must rid himself of his phantoms, and we know that she means that the same thing will happen to her brother as happened to L'Homme if he does not do so. But her advice does little good. Carolles' curiosity is replacing his grief and love. He delights in striving to verify some of the things his wife's phantom has told him. After the strangling of Béatrice by Berthe, however, Albert Carolles permanently loses his equilibrium and becomes the victim of his own curiosity about the supernatural.

The lack of clarity in the symbolism and the weak dramatic construction of the play, as well as its shallow characterizations, make this play one of Lenormand's weakest attempts in the theatre. The play has little significance. Carolles is no more than a dimly indicated exile who retires from life temporarily to unravel the mysteries of his own past, but neither he nor we discover what these mysteries really were.

The influence of climate on the actions and reactions of the characters of Lenormand is another important aspect of his theatre and one in which the problems of the Lenormand hero become more clearly defined. Three of his plays are set exclusively in Africa[85] and two more are partially set there.[86] Two of the plays take place in northern countries,[87] six are set wholly or partially in Switzerland or the French Alps,[88] one in Brittany,[89] one in La Manche,[90] two partially in the Orient.[91] Only one takes place exclusively in Paris.[92]

The influence of climate on an important character is first seen in *Le Temps est un songe*. Nico, having been in the East Indies, finds Holland a stagnant place and feels he, like the people who live near him, is becoming stagnant, too. In contrast the Indies are a relaxing place where one accepts life and does not think too much about it. The stagnancy of Holland and the doubts which arise in Nico's mind because of the mental state communicated by the climate eventually make him commit suicide.

The play, however, in which the characters most experience the evil effects of climate is *Le Simoun*. In this play the desert and its elements take on an almost romantic symbolism. The atmosphere, external nature, not only causes the passions and restlessness of the people but also reflects them, and responds to their moods.

Laurency, the main character of *Le Simoun*, settled in Africa twenty years before the play begins. He left his wife after three months of marriage, still loving her but unable to live with her. His wife has given birth to his daughter, whom Laurency has never seen, but who joins him as the play opens. Because she resembles her mother so strikingly Laurency becomes enamoured of her, and much of the play is concerned with this passion. Its development is skillfully treated and Laurency's unconscious desires are subtly suggested.

Laurency is a man who has been greatly influenced by the climate of the desert. He suggests this himself when he explains to Clotilde, his daughter, the reason for his not taking much interest in her in the early years of her life:

I should have liked to take care of you. . . . It's absurd, contradictory. . . . But when you have lived here a little time you'll understand.[93]

At first the brightness and the silence intoxicate you. . . . In the long run they annoy you. And finally they frighten you.[94]

Like Nico, Laurency has been stagnating in a country which is hostile to his well-being, but he is powerless to leave it, as are the other characters in the play. The problems of these French colonials are much the same as Nico's. They all thirst for the absolute, but Nico, realizing that his thirst can never be assuaged, commits suicide. The Frenchmen have not the courage to act in any manner; they just deteriorate passively. They are the victims of inertia.

When the simoon appears at the end of the play the suppressed passions of the characters find an outlet, as if in sympathy with the storm. Laurency says:

We are like the Thalmoudites. . . . They're a legendary tribe. It is written of them that they lived in rocks sheltered from the storms, surrendered to their passions.[95]

Laurency, who is about to succumb to his incestuous passion for Clotilde, is saved by the storm and by Aïescha, who has murdered the young girl. Like Lenormand's other heroes, Laurency is a completely passive character. He has done nothing to halt his desire for his daughter. Aïescha is the only one who could have saved him. His reaction to his daughter's corpse is psychologically just although rather grotesque:

Laurency still contemplates the corpse but, little by little, his expression changes. It now reflects a sort of animal-like relief, the physical relaxing of the hunted beast who feels himself out of reach.[96]

All the heroes in the theatre of Lenormand are living in a state of anguish, and this condition results from their spiritual alienation. The only solution for them is a passive one of flight from their fate or death, which some of them achieve. It is actually this passivity and flight from reality which deny the Lenormand hero the ability to be tragic. When a man stands up against his fate and battles it, even though the battle be a losing one, we can admire his courage and pity his predicament, but for the characters who flee or hide from their fate or choose suicide as the only way out there is no admiration on the spectator's part.

One strange characteristic of Lenormand's exiles is that they all avoid physical action of any sort. They talk for hours about their problems but never do anything about them. Those who commit murder or suicide or who rob are acting passively. Their acts are not designed to better their condition. Most of the heroes, however, only act mentally, if they are even capable of that. Some are not and they then fall into greater despondency than they would have had they taken some positive course of action. Tragedies have been written about characters who are essentially cerebral, but these characters strive against their fate and do not accept it without having first revolted against it.

Most of Lenormand's characters have aspirations, but the possibility of their attaining their ends is slight because of the diseased character of their personalities. Nico would like to understand the problem of time and existence; Lui in *Les Ratés* would like to become a great writer; his wife would

like to be a well-known actress; the Vérificateur would like
to be able to think less and lose himself in debauchery (a
negative aspiration, but an aspiration just the same); Luc de
Brontë would like to become a great psychiatrist; Sarterre
would like to create a new world of music; Fearon would like
to control the destiny of empires; LaMouette would like to become a woman; André would like to find love with Julie; le
Père Sahler would like to establish the Christian religion in
Africa; but each is defeated before he starts. None of these
characters has the fixity of purpose to attain his goal because
none of them wants one thing only. Their personalities are not
solid enough for them to pursue any one path, except perhaps
the path of evil, which, essentially a negative one, never leads
to the fulfillment of their aspirations. Few of Lenormand's
heroes have the ability to remain in control of themselves,
much less the ability to attain any great distinction.

Fearon again comments on man, and her remarks are per-
tinent to Lenormand's heroes in general:

Tell me what is not mixed up in the heart of man—*All mixed up,
my dear*, jumbled, incoherent, like the wave lengths of the
radio which cross each other in the storm. . . . Oh, if it were
evil, betrayal, or hypocrisy, *all right!—But it's worse!* It's the
cocktail, the mixture, the yellow liquor which flows into the
green . . . and the orange bitters which confuse everything.
Pigs! They don't even know that they're mixed! They think
they're all gin or all vermouth. Pouah! That's why they can't
end anything, succeed in anything, do anything. Oh, let the
world be saved or lost, what the hell, but let there come again
the animal all in one piece—the beast who wants good or the
beast who wants evil—*the real beast!* I'm bored to death seeing
these sick animals, these types of intelligent ghosts, who can
neither live nor die nor create nor destroy, who think, who
think . . . and who don't even know what they're thinking.[97]

No better summary could be made of the Lenormand hero-
exile of the lower depths than these words of Fearon because
they apply to every major character and many of the secondary ones in his eighteen published plays.

None of Lenormand's characters is a great tragic figure.
None of them has any cardinal vices. They are all people in
various stages of mental sickness who cannot adjust to the
rigors of a world which seems hostile to them. We can admire a man whose flaw is his pride, but not one who practices
evil for evil's sake, even though we understand why he does

so. We can pity the man haunted by jealousy, but not one who is a garrulous coward. And all of Lenormand's heroes, interesting as we may find them, fall into the category of special cases of mental psychoses. If Lenormand's theatre is a portrayal of the twentieth century, therefore, the twentieth century must be a dreadful place indeed. And yet several dramatists have found noble people in modern life and have attempted to make tragic figures of them, and, having read their works, we wonder whether Lenormand's picture is a distorted one.

The theatre of Lenormand is depressing; it is a study of the lower depths of man's soul, and there is little light in it. Its subjects, its characters, and its settings are all depressing and its basic pessimism is close to being revolting. There is no catharsis in his plays, only unrelieved tension.

When a ray of light appears in the dark world of the author of *Le Simoun*, it serves only to contrast with the dismal surroundings it lights. If, as Fearon says in *Mixture*, man is a mixture of good and evil, the latter is developed and the former almost ignored in Lenormand's drama. Serge Radine claims that this is because Lenormand's characters are only concrete images of his own personality, that Lenormand's theatre is one of isolation and solitude because Lenormand himself felt his own isolation and solitude. Thus Radine indicates the romantic aspects of Lenormand's personality.[98] Like the romantic author who would not or could not accept the society of his day, Lenormand denies and condemns an epoch in which he feels himself an exile. He therefore peoples his theatre with exiles, and with the most horrible kind, the mental exile who must live with his own doubts and fears, who chooses to disintegrate in solitude or to die rather than to accept help or to help himself.

## CHAPTER IV

# The Sauvage

THE characters of Jean Anouilh's plays are latter-day romantics whose inability or refusal to adjust to their social *milieu*, and consequently to life itself, is the direct cause of their alienation. Throughout Anouilh's plays, in the comedies as well as in the tragedies, similar characters act and react to essentially similar stimuli with almost invariably patterned reflexes which set the Anouilh hero and heroine apart from other figures in modern drama and give to Anouilh's plays their characteristic traits.

Anouilh has divided his earlier plays into two categories, the *pièces roses* and the *pièces noires*, the only difference between the two being that in the former the tone is lighter and the end seldom tragic. In both groups, however, there are the same flights from reality and the same emphasis on the sordidness of the everyday world.

The world as Anouilh sees it is materialistic, a world in which there are only haves and have-nots. In this world social and economic distinctions are of the utmost importance, and a character can seldom move from one social or financial group to another without serious results. The world of the author of *La Sauvage* is a vulgar world, a world of egotists and hypocrites who are interested in their own welfare and who care about others only in proportion to their financial value. Into this world, in each play, steps a young idealist whose quest in this world for an absolute, be it absolute purity or absolute love, is doomed to failure before the action actually starts.

These young idealists, because of their origins, resemble the heroes of many of the nineteenth-century romantic plays. Like Hernani, Ruy Blas, and Antony, Anouilh's characters— Thérèse in *La Sauvage*, Frantz in *L'Hermine*, Eurydice in

*Eurydice*, Marc in *Jézabel*, Georges in *Le Rendez-vous de Senlis*, and Diane in *L'Invitation au château*—have a malediction weighing upon them, a malediction brought about by their origins. Jacques Carot calls this malediction the fatality of origins, and comments that most of the Anouilh characters have "a precocious seriousness which they owe to their severe experience."[1] Most of these characters are of lower bourgeois origin. Their parents are usually vulgar, ineffectual, interested only in money and maintaining a false and ridiculous pride. Their "fistons" and "fifilles" generally despise them for their bad qualities and try to revolt against them. These young idealists try to elevate themselves in the world in their quest for purity, but, with few exceptions, they are unable to do so because their very origins act as a kind of psychological deterrent to action.

The poverty of the families from which most of the Anouilh characters arise gives the heroes and heroines an unjust and over-magnified conception of the power of money. To Frantz, as to many others in the plays, money means purity or the state in which purity can be obtained. In the Anouilh vocabulary wealth is the exact opposite of the vulgarity and vice which are the chief adjuncts of poverty. In *Jézabel* Jacqueline tells Marc:

We would go to live in the country. I am rich. It's shameful to say, but you would see how with a little money everything becomes easy.[2]

Money, at least in the early Anouilh plays, thus becomes a symbol of happiness and success. And yet excessive riches do not mean happiness either, as Florent discovers in *La Sauvage* and Diane finds in *L'Invitation au château*. One must have enough money to live in moderate comfort but not so much that one is out of contact with life. In the later plays, however, Anouilh seems to show that money in itself is bad, as is the economic system caused by its worship. The inequalities brought about by this system are, he feels, only too often the reason for tragedy in our society.

Perhaps because of their miserable childhoods the Anouilh characters aim high. They want perfection but once they attain it or even something approximating it they are impotent to accept it because their past will not permit them to do so. Frantz yearns for money so that he can marry Monime and find perfect love with her. Once he has killed Monime's

aunt, however, he realizes that he will never have the love
which he has been seeking and therefore chooses to die.
Antigone, seeking perfection, knows that it will mean her
death, but she will not compromise. Thérèse is unable to live
happily with Florent and, although this marriage could mean
happiness to her, she is unable, because of her past, to
accept it.

The seeking of perfection by the Anouilh heroes illumi-
nates the anti-social aspect of his theatre. For the author of
*Antigone*, the man who is like other men is vile and worthy
of scorn.[3] He is accepting implicitly the villainy and hypocrisy of society and making virtues of them. Ludovic in *Y
avait un prisonnier* exemplifies this attitude. He sees the
hypocrisy and petty weaknesses of his family and refuses
to become like them. He will not accept society because
society is corrupt and yet in Anouilh's theatre society has no
place for the exceptional or sensitive person, and thus these
people invariably become failures or exiles because of society's
scorn.

Poverty exposes the Anouilh hero to another characteristic
aspect of alienation, solitude. Whether the characters are
poor or not, however, they all partake of an inner loneliness
which sets them apart from other people. The older characters
experience this solitude in a rather pathetic fashion. Age
in Anouilh's theatre almost invariably means loss of sexual
potency, and consequently age implies loss of sexual companions. There is no compensation for the sexual decline.

The older men and women in these plays are seldom
happy. They are almost all victims of a nostalgia that causes
them to live in a past which is all too often seen through mis-
focused eyes. Créon, Orphée's father, Lady Hurff, the father
in *Roméo et Jeannette*, Tarde, Marc's mother, are all lonely
people to whom age has brought no rewards. Lady Hurff
sums up the feelings of the older Anouilh characters when
she says:

I have had all that a woman can reasonably and even unreason-
ably wish. Money, power, lovers. Now that I am old I find
myself just as lonely as when I was a little girl who was stood
in the corner as penance. And what is more serious, I realize
that between that little girl and this old woman there was, with
a good deal of commotion, only a still worse solitude.[4]

If the older characters in Anouilh's theatre feel their essential loneliness, the younger ones experience it even more so. Antigone might be speaking for Marc or Thérèse or Frantz or Georges when she says: "Animals huddle together to keep warm. I am all alone."[5]

All the means for escaping this solitude are vain. Orphée discovers that love only increases his loneliness because, "in the long run it is horrible to be two."[6]

One way in which most of the Anouilh heroes try to conquer their solitude is through friendship. Georges in *Le Rendez-vous de Senlis* invents an imaginary friend and endows him with the most admirable qualities. Gaston in *Le Voyageur sans bagages* seeks for a childhood friend who, rather than one of his former mistresses, might help him regain his memory. Ludovic turns to his friend, Marcellin, for help in *Y avait un prisonnier*. But each of these fails. The friend, the ideal friendship, never materializes, and each of the characters is as lonely as before.

If the characters experience solitude, however, they are still part of a group, usually a family group. Anouilh advocates, as Gide did earlier, breaking all ties with one's family. And yet the family in Anouilh's theatre is drawn together by bonds which are apparently unbreakable. No matter how hard one tries one can seldom break away from one's family. One's past makes him one of them. What seems to join the members of a family is a bad conscience or the weight of communal faults or the desire for mutual exploitation.[7] Thérèse, Marc, Gustave, Julia, and Frantz are bound to their families for these reasons. Each tries to break away from the family group of which he is a part, and each fails signally. His past is too much with him.

Each character in Anouilh's theatre would like to be able to cut himself off completely from his past, but only one, Gaston, is able to do so, and he can do it only because he is a victim of amnesia. The solution to the problem of being forced to live with one's past is death, and many of Anouilh's characters choose death. Créon sees that Antigone was made for death and Antigone does everything possible to verify Créon's assumption. Frantz, Orphée, Eurydice, Jeannette, Frédérick, and Médée choose death. Gaston, by killing the person of Jacques Renaud, murders his past symbolically. Ludovic and Marc choose to disappear, a fact which could also be interpreted as symbolical death since they are denying their pasts.

The conflict in Anouilh's theatre is always between accepted order and exile, or idealism which effects the exile; and the established order always wins. Antigone defies Créon, who is a symbol of convention, and dies. Frantz, Thérèse, Médée, and Marc try to revolt against society and they fail. Ludovic and Georges attempt to defy the social structure and they become exiled from it. This failure of the heroes in their battle against convention and order gives Anouilh's theatre its definitely pessimistic tone.

All the heroes and heroines of Anouilh's drama are what he himself has called some of them—*sauvages*. They are related in some respects to the eighteenth century's noble savage and to the romantic ideal of the man whose own nature is more important than convention. Each of Anouilh's heroes is, or is meant to be, an intrinsically fine and noble person. Each revolts (even if the revolt is merely verbal) against the corruption of a materialistic society. Most of these heroes and heroines have powerful feelings of guilt which make the phrase "I am ashamed"[8] almost a trademark of Anouilh's drama, and it is an awareness of this sense of guilt which separates them from the noble savage. They are, however, twentieth-century savages who, in their quest for the absolute, deny life and worship the unobtainable, often without having either the strength of character or the drive necessary to accomplish their ends.

These *sauvages* have several other traits which relate them to the eighteenth-century ideal. Most of them, although they come from sordid backgrounds, look upon their childhood as a time of purity, of perfection. This innocence of childhood lasted until someone made them aware of the grotesqueness of life: Marc met his mother with one of her lovers. Thérèse realized her parents thought of her as a barterable object. Yet each Anouilh hero idolizes childhood innocence and purity, and one, Georges, even invents a happy childhood.

But if they have had or would like to have had a childhood of innocence, most of the characters have never had what should follow chronologically immediately after it—adolescence. Marc's mother informs him, "You have never been like others. As a child you were as serious and sure of yourself as a man."[9] This is true of most of the other heroes and heroines, too. Like Marc, Amanda, Georges, Thérèse, Jeannette, Gustave, and Frantz had to fend for themselves at an early age, with the result that they almost matured over-night—almost, because none of these people ever really did mature. Having bypassed adolescence as others experience it, they seem, in their twenties and thirties to be reverting to that state which they should have passed through years before. Thus their actions and reactions often seem immature. In Anouilh's theatre it seems almost as if adolescence can never be repressed completely. If it is ignored or bypassed in the teens it will make itself evident at a later age with results that are often unfortunate. This is shown most clearly in their attitude toward love. Love, to them, is something mysterious and divine; it includes intercourse but seldom emphasizes it. Unlike the love of their parents, the love of the young heroes and heroines has nothing vulgar about it but neither does it have much reality. Time and again the men call the girls their little brothers, or the women call their lovers "mon capitaine" or describe their love as comradeship. Too often this makes one think of the puppy love of the middle teens, a sort of comradeship from which a mature sex relationship is absent. This emotional adolescence as well as the heroes' search for purity and their unbreakable idealism give the Anouilh characters an aura of immaturity and make his heroines seem like young girls rather than women.

*L'Hermine* is the first published play of Anouilh and in it the character of the *sauvage* hero-exile is clearly indicated. Frantz, the son of the doctor of the Duchesse de Granat, has been raised by her as an impoverished child in an atmosphere of luxury. The Duchesse constantly reminds him of his lack of wealth and social status but she tries to marry him to a woman of wealth. Frantz, however, is in love with Monime, the niece of the Duchesse, and she with him, but because of the opposition of the old woman to this marriage Frantz decides he must have money in order to elope with Monime. To Frantz money symbolizes happiness; and the possession of wealth will bring him to that state of purity to which all the Anouilh heroes and heroines aspire. Frantz is, however, unable to borrow the money from M. Bentz and, because his happiness depends on wealth, he decides to break the laws of society and murder the Duchesse so that Monime will inherit her aunt's fortune. He murders the old woman but Monime is horrified by the act and refuses to marry him. Realizing that happiness is now impossible, Frantz confesses the crime.

Being a poor man, Frantz feels his exile strongly:

Frantz:     . . . I have discovered what a sinister farce a poor childhood was.
Philippe:   A very wealthy childhood is a farce too.
Frantz:     I know; no contact with life. The poor invented that to console themselves. They did not say what it was to be a young man at whom women do not smile. A young man who doesn't know how to speak to head waiters and whose every natural gesture is studied.[10]

This passage also indicates rather forcefully the characteristic weakness of the Anouilh *sauvage*. The *sauvage* is the natural man who is alienated because he cannot assume the artificial exterior society demands. He is someone who sees the injustices of the social system under which he lives; but, rather than try to change that social system, he just tries to ameliorate his own condition, a nearly impossible task in Anouilh's theatre. Frantz differs from Thérèse of *La Sauvage* in this respect. He longs for the life of the wealthy man which he has seen only from the outside whereas Thérèse comes to see the life of the wealthy from the inside and refuses it.

Throughout the play Frantz is alone. He has become alienated from his friends in his own social group and he always feels his financial separation from the people of Monime's class. Even Monime's presence does not make him feel less lonely. He regards her as a "have" while he is a "have not." Monime is willing to run away with him and live in poverty but he refuses this sacrifice. She would regret it and eventually would hate him for it because poverty will become the ally of their enemies. Frantz feels that he can love Monime only when they will be protected by money. His love is pure, and he does not want it soiled; without money their love will certainly be sullied,[11] and yet, paradoxically, money is the symbol of dirtiness, and thus there appears to be no escape from dirtiness.

If Frantz feels alone with Monime before he murders her aunt, he is even more alone afterwards. He, the *sauvage*, seeking something beyond the limits of human nature, has broken the laws of society and must suffer accordingly and in solitude.

Jean Didier claims, and justifiably, that Frantz is a romantic hero, without illusions, because all of his life he has been in the grips of material misery whereas his predecessors in the nineteenth century were in the clutches of difficulties of sentiment or morality.[11]

If Frantz is essentially a romantic hero without illusions, Thérèse, the heroine of *La Sauvage*, is even more a romantic at grips with an avowedly unsympathetic world. Frantz is not a completely believable character; his lack of remorse after murdering the Duchesse and his incredibly overweening pride make him often seem less than human. Thérèse, on the other hand, is a creature who is only too human.

Thérèse plays the violin in a fifth-rate orchestra conducted by her father, a vulgar man with little to recommend him. She has been brought up in a sordid atmosphere, and yet somehow an aura of purity lingers about her. She has fallen in love with a wealthy, successful, young, and happy pianist, Florent, who returns her love. She has consented to marry him, and after a few debasing scenes with her family goes away with him. She deliberately degrades herself in his eyes and eventually leaves him, unable to adjust to an atmosphere which is not hers.

The opposition of backgrounds in *La Sauvage* causes much of the ensuing tragedy. Thérèse has been reared in an atmosphere of poverty. She has seen all the horrors of life and has experienced much of life's degradation. Florent, being born to a wealthy family, has never known a moment's unhappiness and has always had whatever he wanted. Thérèse, when she enters the world of Florent, brings with her feelings of guilt. She is ashamed of her parents, of the *milieu* in which she has been brought up, of her past experiences. She resents the advantages which have made of Florent the person he is, and is jealous of him. Florent represents unconsciously to Thérèse the perfection which she desires but knows she can never attain; her past forbids it.

She feels that Florent is ignorant of life and yet she always feels guilty when she is with him because she can never be other than she is, a product of her environment. When she sees him cry, however, and knows he is crying because she is leaving him, she realizes that he too can suffer and be unhappy. She therefore decides to marry him. She assures herself that she will be of some use to him, that he needs her. But when she discovers that he takes her marrying him for granted she knows that she cannot remain. She would be betraying her ideals, and consequently she wanders off into the night.

Thérèse, like Frantz, has an ideal of purity, but, to her,

money does not represent this purity. She claims she is "de cette race,"[12] the race to which her parents and intimates belong, the race for which everything is represented by money. Essentially, however, she is interested only in her own ideal of purity and her happiness. Edward Marsh explains the nature of this purity towards which Thérèse is struggling:

> Thérèse's character is one of pure revolt. Reason, inclination and good luck all point the easy way. Against all these she defends her integrity—an integrity wounded but made more sensitive and compassionate by experience. Her sense of what is *fitting*—what sort of happiness she is capable of enjoying and giving—decides her actions. This sense is something pure and fine which is in touch with life at a point beyond considerations of justice and happiness; by it she apprehends a meaning or pattern in life, a purity which has its own laws in relation to each individual soul. The ordinary pursuit of justice and happiness dulls this sense in most people, dulls them to the deeper knowledge of the "fitting." Thérèse preserves it intact. Ordinary notions of happiness are irrelevances. Happiness in any sense is irrelevant. It is only this sense of the purity by which her soul will remain whole that can give life a meaning and direction.[13]

Thérèse, in deciding to leave Florent, performs an act which in itself is worthy of admiration. Like most romantics, she is forced to live in an environment which she detests and from which, while she lives, she cannot escape. She has ideals of purity and yet cannot see herself as pure. She longs for the infinite and yet is aware that she is mortal. She is caught in a duality of affirmation and negation: consequently her disappearing from both the social group of Florent and her own *milieu* is the only solution. In this act, however, she affirms the existence of a purity which has its own laws over and beyond those of human nature. At the same time she must deny, and in this respect she comes close to being tragic, a corrupt world which prevents her from attaining her purity. What ultimately prevents Thérèse from having the stature of a tragic figure is that she is damned because there *is* original sin but unfortunately no grace, and her affirmation of purity therefore seems less meaningful.

Throughout the play Thérèse realizes her isolation. She is spiritually alienated from her family and the people of her own *milieu*. Yet when she moves to the society of Florent she feels alienated because she thinks of herself as being too representative of her lower middle-class origins. Feeling strongly about her status in Florent's house, she says: "I tremble at being the only one here who does not know how to smile, the only one soiled by life, the only poor one, the only shameful one."[14]

In the first act of the play, she looks upon her family with poorly contained disgust, yet in the second act she does everything possible to make herself, her family, and her rearing seem abhorrent to Florent. She becomes a veritable savage, completely destructive, negative, attacking everything which might possibly be conceived of as having to do with society, and in so doing she inevitably furthers her own isolation from that society.

Her revolt against Florent's love and against his way of life is as complete as her revolt against her family. She will not accept assistance or advice from anyone. She tells Hartman that her troubles are her own, that he should busy himself with his own, if he has any. She feels her solitude and yet believes that no one can understand her. She does want to be happy; she assures us of this several times. But if happiness is her goal, she is powerless to achieve it. Only love might make her forget her sense of degradation; and the man whom she loves is the very one who cannot help her because he is ignorant of what life is; he has never experienced shame and degradation himself. She therefore runs away because, as she tells Hartman,[15] there will always be a stray dog somewhere in the world to keep her from being happy. She is sure that her sense of loneliness will be even more acute if she marries Florent than if she disappears.

Understanding the meaning of *sauvage* is crucial to an understanding of Anouilh's theatre. A *sauvage* is a person who, like Antigone, says, "I am here to say no."[16] This type of person will not accept the society of which he is a part not only because that society is corrupt and hypocritical, but because his own longings for purity make him refuse to compromise with man and the world in which he lives. He therefore denies society and destroys himself, always with what he considers to be justification, because he has an ideal to which he will remain faithful come what may. Dying for ideals may be, and often is, tragic in the works of Sophocles and Shakespeare, but the ideals are more specific and human—honor, love, etc.—than are the transcendental and never completely realized ideals of purity of Anouilh's characters.

Eurydice, the next important heroine of Anouilh, is also a *sauvage* who has much in common with her fellow heroes and heroines. Like many of them she places little faith in the perfection of human love. Like most of them she has been brought up in a rather sordid atmosphere from which she is never able to escape. As with Thérèse, her past is always present, and she cannot deny it.

Eurydice does not have the pure ideal of love subscribed to by Orphée. She is uncertain about the permanence of love. One of the first things she tells Orphée when she meets him in a railroad station buffet is that she will be terribly unhappy and very alone when he leaves her.[17] She is as uncertain of her own emotions as she is of Orphée's, and she betrays a childlike innocence in making him swear that he will never leave her. Her very search for perfect love, and her consequent awareness that such love does not exist short of death, eventually causes her to leave Orphée.

The whole quality of their love is adolescent. Here perhaps more than in any other of Anouilh's plays we find the teen-age love which is so characteristic of the lovers in his theatre. They speak of themselves as being comrades;[18] Orphée becomes the captain and Eurydice the follower;[19] they speak of themselves as being two little brothers.[20] The purity and the ideal quality of their relationship do not seem sufficiently real or tragic in a broad human sense, because of this juvenile atmosphere. And yet, because of the gravity with which they take their affair, their love becomes rather terrifying.

Eurydice, however, will never achieve her ideal love with Orphée because of previous sex experiences to which she has been subjected. She feels tainted and therefore unworthy of Orphée's love. Like Thérèse she has immortal longings and a mortal body, and therefore there is little hope for her in this world since, as Anouilh says in a curiously Sartrian manner, one can never become another; living is an accumulation of past shames and sins. Because Eurydice is unable to support the weight of truth about her past, and fears repetition of the past in the future, she dies, not only accidentally on a bus, but symbolically with Orphée.

Both Eurydice and Orphée sense their loneliness. Orphée at first is terribly sure of his love and his ideal. Eurydice resents this in much the same manner as Thérèse resents the self-satisfaction of Florent. It makes her feel the weight of her past more strongly, and she thus seems less worthy in her own eyes. She tells Orphée:

Ah! You can be carefree—yes—now that you have weighted me down. . . . You say things, you bring back to life all those sordid couples who made love between these four walls at the moment one least expects it. You smear us with sticky old words and then forget them. You descend to dinner saying it's a delightful evening, there are lights everywhere, there's a delicious odor of garlic.[21]

Orphée does not really believe that Eurydice is worried or unhappy until after she leaves him and then the revelation overwhelms the youth. He realizes that purity or his ideal love (which is the equivalent of purity in *Eurydice*) is impossible in this world. He says despairingly, "Because in the long run being two is intolerable."[22] It is at this moment that he becomes aware of what the other Anouilh characters know instinctively, that man is always alone with himself and that only in death is there a perfect consummation.

As in the classical legend, Orphée, through the medium of a M. Henri who represents death, is given back Eurydice on condition that he not look at her before daybreak. But Orphée's love is idealistic and he must know everything and therefore he must look into Eurydice's heart. But the ideal and the mortal cannot co-exist; one negates the other and Orphée sees that his ideal is unattainable on earth. Having killed Eurydice by looking at her, he commits suicide. Living to the lovers means compromising with truth, and neither will accept this. Instead they choose death, which here again is the negation of a sordid and second-rate existence which the *sauvage* will not tolerate. At the same time death is an affirmation of their love.

The parallel in the play between the love of Orphée and Eurydice and that of Eurydice's mother and her lover, Vincent, is striking. The mother and Vincent have compromised their ideals and consequently their love is vulgar not only to the young lovers but to the audience. Eurydice feels that her love for Orphée would descend to this vulgarity eventually, and finds this to be an intolerable thought. When his father recounts his sordid affairs of former days, Orphée has much the same reaction. The play ends, therefore, pessimistically, with a complete negation of life and the avowed impossibility of a pure love in this world. In *Eurydice* Anouilh demonstrates that love is impossible even when experienced by members of the same social station. Thérèse and Florent were separated by the differences in their backgrounds and therefore their love was doomed to failure. Orphée and Eurydice are of the same class, but their intimate experiences and reactions are different. Only in death can lovers become one.

Eurydice is the more destructive force in this play because it is she who destroys Orphée's illusions. Realizing she will never be able to attain purity, she disappears, as Thérèse does, without even a word of farewell. Both realize that the struggle for purity is hopeless because they cannot break the chains which tie them to their past. Since they will not accept compromise, the word hope does not exist for them. Hope only prolongs a useless fight. M. Henri sums up the plight of Thérèse, Orphée, and Eurydice as well as most of the other Anouilh heroes and heroines when he tells Orphée, "You're all the same. You thirst for eternity."[23] And only in death is their thirst assuaged.

What Thérèse and Eurydice have refused or been unable to do, namely to break the ties which connected them with their past, Gaston, the hero of *Le Voyageur sans bagages*, does. Gaston is a man of thirty-five who has spent the eighteen years previous to the time of the play in a rest home. He is a victim of amnesia; he was injured in the First World War. Because he has become a sort of national enigma, his doctor and the doctor's aunt have decided to find his family. They hope that by having Gaston live with several families, which may be his, certain memories of the past will emerge and cure him of his malady. The first of the families to which Gaston is sent is the wealthy bourgeois Renaud family which consists of a mother, a son, and a daughter-in-law. They know immediately that Gaston is their son and brother, Jacques, and they try to convince him of this. Gaston finds them to be rather repulsive people. His horror, however, is not confined to the revelation of their characters but springs chiefly from the emerging character of the young Jacques Renaud who they try to convince him he was.

Gaston is a humble and contented, if not a happy, man. In the rest home he was without commitments and responsibilities, and he enjoyed this status.[24] With the Renauds, however, he will commit himself and take on responsibilities if he is proved to be their son. This would not annoy him, however, if he discovered that his childhood was one of innocence and purity.

But among thousands of possible memories it is precisely the memory of a friend that I conjured up with the most longing. I have built everything on the memory of that imaginary friend. Our inspiring walks, the books we had discovered together, a girl we had both loved at the same time and whom I had sacrificed to him, and even—you're going to laugh—that I had saved his life one day while we were boating.[25]

But Jacques Renaud was a little monster. He tortured and killed animals. He slapped his mother. He pushed his best friend down the stairs and broke his back in an argument over a chambermaid. Gaston hears these things with horror, and the horror is even greater because he knows that he really is Jacques Renaud. As a youth he had seduced his brother's wife, Valentine, who recognizes him because of a scar on his back. This assures both Gaston and us that he is Jacques. Valentine tells him that he must accept himself as he is. Gaston cannot do this, however, as Thérèse and Eurydice are forced to do. In order to live he has to kill someone, and that someone is Jacques Renaud. He tells Valentine that it is his privilege to refuse to be Jacques:

I am doubtless the only man, it's true, to whom fate will have given the possibility of accomplishing each man's dream. . . . I am a man and I can be, if I will it, as unspoiled as a new-born child. That's a privilege which it would be criminal not to take advantage of. I refuse you. Since yesterday I have had only too many things to forget about myself.[26]

Valentine informs Gaston that he cannot escape, he cannot refuse. He has no choice other than returning to the rest home. But fate intervenes and helps Gaston. One of the families which has come to claim him consists only of a young boy, all of whose relatives have been drowned at sea. Gaston accepts being the boy's nephew and leaves with him. Edward Marsh says, "this dénouement is entirely in keeping with the rebellious and self-centered character of Jacques Renaud."[27] A horrible thought! Yet it helps to demonstrate Anouilh's contention that one can never completely escape from one's past.

Jacques Renaud was a negative force, a destroyer, yet many of his characteristics may be seen in Gaston who, like many other Anouilh characters, has an ideal of purity. Gaston's reactions to the mother are almost exactly the same as Jacques' had been eighteen years before.[28] There is the same two-sidedness in Gaston's character as in that of Frantz or Antigone or Eurydice. Yet he is apparently able to compromise with life as they are not. Consequently his happiness, which at the end of the play seems unconvincing and preconceived, is not admirable because he is running away from life in order to begin again. His choice, therefore, is just as negative as that of his predecessors in the theatre of Anouilh.

Antigone, perhaps the best known of Anouilh's heroines, is also a *sauvage* but she differs in one important respect from her fellow heroes and heroines. Eurydice, Thérèse, Gaston, and Georges in the *Rendez-vous de Senlis* cannot tolerate the past, with the result that the future becomes intolerable for them. Antigone, and here she resembles Frantz more than any other Anouilh personality, cannot face the future. Antigone is a *sauvage* who refuses to accept the ordinary conditions of life and therefore seeks death. She is the personification of youthful idealism which will admit no compromise (as Créon had been paradoxically when he was young). Créon says that she was made to die and she does seek death. She negates a life which to her is false and hypocritical and on which she feels men unjustifiably base a meaningless happiness.

Anouilh's play resembles the Sophoclean original in many respects. In Anouilh's *Antigone*, as in Sophocles' play, the tragic emphasis is placed upon Créon. The established order in Anouilh's play, as represented by Créon, is symbolical of life in Paris in 1940 under the heel of the Nazi conquerors. Créon could easily be said to represent collaboration.

He has accepted what Antigone considers to be false values. She tells him he could have refused to take over the helm when the ship of state was foundering. Créon feels that this would have been a completely negative act. He claims that one must accept responsibility and say yes, no matter how shameful the consequences may be; one must accept everything therefore:

To say yes, one must sweat and roll up his sleeves, seize life with both hands and plunge in up to the elbows. It's easy to say no, even if one must die. One has only to stand one's ground and wait. Wait to live, even wait to be killed. That's too cowardly. It's a fabrication of man. Can you imagine a world in which the trees too have denied the sap, in which animals have denied the hunting or mating instinct? Animals, at least, are good and simple and tough. They go, crowding each other, forward, one after the other, courageously, on the same road. And if they fall, others will tread over them, and no matter how many fall there will still always remain one of each species ready to bring forth young and continue along the same road with the same courage, exactly like those who have gone before.[29]

Créon, even if his analogies are not sound, defends, as will Colombe ten years later, the debasing kind of life Anouilh has heretofore attacked viciously. But his words have little effect on Antigone who is not interested in compromise. If she cannot have purity she would rather die. She would like to live, however; she says so several times. But living for her is really only surviving.[30] It is experiencing the joys of the young animal who is sensitive to the exterior world. But, of course, it is also retaining the purity of childhood and existing in a never-never land of idealism. Antigone knows that living this way is really impossible. She can never re-experience the innocence of childhood; therefore she will die. Créon does his best to convince her that death would be ridiculous. He proves to the young girl (she already knows this anyway) that the burial of Polynice is nothing but religious charlatanism. The argument which almost succeeds in swaying her is the fact that Etéocle was just as bad as Polynice and that Créon is not even sure which of the brothers has been buried. He demonstrates that her gesture of loyalty is ridiculous because neither of the brothers was worth much anyway. Antigone is swayed by this argument and probably would have accepted Créon's decree if he had not made the mistake of lecturing her and giving her his views of life. Horrified by his practicality, Antigone decides that death is preferable to his life of compromise which is devoid of the purity she has been seeking:

> You all disgust me with your happiness! With your life that one must love no matter what the cost. Like dogs who lick everything they find. And that bit of luck, for every day if one doesn't ask too much. I want everything, immediately—and I want it complete—or I refuse. I don't want to be modest and content myself with a scrap if I have been a good girl. I want to be sure of everything today, and I want it to be as fine as when I was a child—or else die.[31]

Créon orders the execution of Antigone, and because her death affirms her belief in an ideal, impractical though it may

be, one may assume that the theme of the play is that purity
can be attained only in death.

Throughout the play Antigone is alone. The prologue
tells us that, ". . . she is going to rise up suddenly from the
thin, swarthy and withdrawn girl that no one in the family
took seriously and rise up alone against the world, alone
against Créon, her uncle, who is the king."[32] Her loneliness
and exile become more horrible as the action progresses until
at the end she is almost unable to bear them herself. When
she leaves the stage with the guard, going to her death, her
loneliness overwhelms her and even she is not sure why she
is dying.

During the play the chorus discourses upon tragedy and
claims that in tragedy there is never hope:

In tragedy we are calm. First of all we understand each other.
We are all innocents in short! It's not because there's one
who kills and another who is killed. It's a question of casting.
And then, above all, tragedy is restful because we know there is
no more hope, deceptive hope; that we are caught, that we are
finally caught like a rat with all the gods against us, that all cries,
groans, complaints are useless now, that it is useless to shout out
what we had to say, what we had never said and what we
perhaps didn't even know yet. And to no avail, just for the
sake of saying it to ourselves, to make ourselves fully aware
of it.[33]

If this is not true with regard to all tragedy, and this point
is certainly debatable, it is true in Anouilh's plays. In the
pièces noires there is never any hope. The characters are
damned the moment they appear on stage, and most of them
know before they have come to grips with their problem
that there is no such thing as hope. Hope only prolongs a
useless battle; it is better to die than to expect that something better will happen. One has either the extreme of
happiness, which is almost unknown in Anouilh's theatre, or
the extreme of misery and death. Only in death is it possible
to find the purity which his young idealists seek; only in death
is there meaning.

One of the most important reasons for the aura of pessimism about the plays is that one of the elements lacking in the
psychological makeup of the Anouilh hero and heroine is hope.
Even Créon, who, albeit a king, might be said to represent
the average person, is not happy and is just as alone as Antigone. Thus Anouilh's theatre becomes a demonstration of

solitude, individual and collective, of shame and degradation, of pessimism and death. Even in the *pièces roses* where the outcome is not tragic, the lightness of treatment does not hide the underlying horror of the daily existence of the heroes and heroines. In the comedies life continues but it is one of doubt and resignation, never one of complete happiness. Even in the later Anouilh of *La Valse des toréadors* the protagonists seem overwhelmed by their own solitude and guilt.

The pathetic aspect of Anouilh's *sauvages* is their youth. To have lost faith in everything at such an early age, and to feel the uselessness of life, to negate existence, in short, is a horrible commentary on the contemporary world.

There seems to be no hope in it, short of death, for the idealist. The world is corrupt and nothing can change it. Because of this, Anouilh's heroes and heroines die what appear to be meaningless deaths. Their very affirmation that only in death can purity be found seems to indicate that life itself has little meaning and certainly very little hope. This would seem to be one of the major reasons for the pessimism in Anouilh's theatre. The battle between his heroes and humanity is weighted heavily on the side of the latter, as it is not in classical tragedy. Thérèse, Antigone, Eurydice, Orphée, and Gaston are idealists who, although painted grey by their creator, fight with a social hydra which is portrayed as completely black. Their defeat by this hydra and their consequent deaths, whether real or symbolic, do not justify man or the universe. These heroes therefore appear to become isolated examples of a revolt which seems personally necessary for them but which showers only the most unflattering commentaries on existence.

These heroes and heroines are certainly more admirable than those of Lenormand because they are not ultimately passive. They *choose* death and, in the eyes of the world, defeat, and, pessimistic as are the connotations of their deaths, they have at least proved themselves able to act: they have not passively accepted *la condition humaine*.

Of all the exiles in the modern French theatre the *sauvages* of Anouilh are the most pathetic and the most frightening. They are the only exiles who completely deny life, the only ones for whom the word hope does not exist. Even Lia in Giraudoux's *Sodome et Gomorrhe* makes an attempt at saving herself and those around her. The Anouilh *sauvages* because of their concern for their personal salvation make no such attempt.

CHAPTER V

# The Implacable Heroines of Giraudoux

GIRAUDOUX is the only contemporary French playwright, with
the possible exception of Paul Claudel, who has created a
dramatic world at all comparable to those of the great dramatists of the past. His world contains people from all social
classes and all educational levels, and whether they be ancient
Greeks, Biblical characters, or provincial Frenchmen, they
transcend their times and become as universal in significance
as any characters in the modern drama.

The men in Giraudoux's theatre are often brilliantly portrayed, and many of them are memorable characters, but the
women of the author of *Amphitryon 38* are his more startling
and also more curious creations. In his last novel, *Choix des
élues*, one of Giraudoux's characters describes what he considers *woman* to be:

The true woman is rare. Most men marry a mediocre counterfeit of men, a little craftier, a bit more lissome, a bit more
beautiful, marry themselves. They see themselves pass in the
street with a little more breast, a little more hip, the whole
wrapped up for their personal pleasure in silk jersey, then they
pursue themselves, kiss themselves and marry themselves. It's
less cold, after all, than marrying a mirror. The true woman is
strong; she strides over obstacles, she overthrows thrones, she
makes time stand still. Her flesh is marble. When there is one,
she is the world's impasse. . . . Where do rivers, clouds, solitary
birds go? To woman. . . . But she is rare. . . . One must flee when
one sees her, for, if she loves, if she hates, she is implacable.
Her compassion is implacable. . . . But she is rare. . . .[1]

The implacable women of whom Giraudoux speaks in this
passage become the heroines of his drama. Geneviève, Andro-
maque, Alcmène, Judith, Ondine, Electre, Isabelle, Lia, Auré-

lie, Lucile are all *women*. They are natural; and yet they appear to be almost superhuman because they are terrifyingly consistent; nothing will stop them once they have made a decision. They are frank; they always say exactly what they mean regardless of the consequences. They are pure because, as Kierkegaard says, purity of heart is to will one thing. They are exact opposites of Lenormand's characters because they do what no Lenormand hero can—will one thing.

Whether she is a virgin or married, the heroine of Giraudoux feels her mission in life. She dislikes hypocrisy and injustice, and, in order to triumph over them, she will let cities burn and men be killed. An abstract idea means more to her than a living reality. Like Hugo's Hernani, the heroine of Giraudoux is "une force qui va."

Each of these heroines has an incredible power of intuition. Like Hélène, she sees only objects that really exist. The superfluous and unimportant details mean nothing to her. Hélène, even more than her sister-in-law, Cassandre, can foretell the future; Judith can see her approaching sainthood; Electre can see the triumph of her justice; Ondine knows that Hans will deceive her; Lia knows that God will destroy Sodom and Gomorrah. Like Sartre's Oreste, each has a mission in life, and yet because of devotion to that mission each heroine seems less human and more the embodiment of some external force or some ideal which obsesses the playwright than she might otherwise seem.

Each of these heroines is alienated, figuratively as well as in reality, from her world but the alienation is more pronounced in some than in others. All of them have some relationship with extra-terrestrial forces and this makes not only their presence, but also the presence of injustice and misfortune in their world apparent to the destiny or fatality which broods over Giraudoux's plays. A transparency of character and what one might almost term an exhibitionistic compulsion make these women different from other people, and, in most cases, this transparency is the direct cause of their alienation. The moment these heroines declare themselves (to borrow an expression used in *Electre*) something tragic happens. Some of them, such as Hélène and Lia, make themselves and their missions apparent immediately. Others grow in importance as the plays progress, and, at the end of each play, there is almost always a woman of larger-than-life stature who dominates the climax. Judith becomes a saint; Electre finds her justice; Ondine tries to save Hans; Lia watches the end of the world; Aurélie disposes of the evil forces in Paris; Hélène remains in Troy; Alcmène proves a bourgeois existence to be preferable to a celestial one.

Claude-Edmonde Magny notes in her excellent volume on Giraudoux that for him the universe is a masked ball, and that therefore metaphysically we can not be sure of finding the definitive truth about anything in the universe.[2] Throughout the plays there are characters who impersonate others, or who do not know their own identity such as Siegfried, Jupiter, Mercure, Egon, Suzanne, Ondine's "parents," Oreste, the Mendiant in *Electre*, the Illusioniste, the Spectre. Most of these characters have important functions in the plays. The impersonation of Egon destroys Judith's pride; Suzanne is a mirror of Judith; the Illusioniste, the Spectre, Jupiter, and Mercure precipitate dramatic action. The Mendiant serves as chorus in *Electre*. Each is important because each in a direct or refracted manner helps emphasize the alienation of the heroine.

Another characteristic of Giraudoux's theatre, and one which magnifies the heroines' sense of alienation is the role played by fate. Each heroine is overwhelmed by a destiny of frightening weight, and this destiny is the motivating action of the plays. Because of it the Trojan War will take place, Judith will sacrifice herself, Electre will cause the ruin of Argos, Sodom and Gomorrah will burn, Isabelle's communications with the Spectre will up set a whole town. That there are certain human beings who are in contact with this fatality is explained by Egisthe in *Electre*:

I do believe in the gods. Or rather, I believe I believe in the gods. But I believe in them, not as great caretakers and great watchmen, but as great abstractions. Between space and time, always oscillating between gravitation and emptiness, there are the great indifferences. Those are the gods. I imagine them, not constantly concerned with that moving mould on the earth which is humanity, but as having reached the stage of serenity and universality. That is blessedness, the same thing as unconsciousness. They are unconscious at the top of the ladder of being, as the atom is at the bottom. The difference is that theirs is the unconsciousness of lightning, omniscient, thousand-faceted, so that in their normal state, like diamonds, powerless and deaf, they only *react* to light, to omens, without understanding them.[3]

In *Electre* and *Intermezzo* it is the heroine who makes the sign. The moment she does, destiny is put in motion. The heroines of the various plays then become either this fatality itself or its instrument and, in so doing, alienate themselves further from the human condition. Hélène has been put on earth by fate for its personal use. Judith becomes her own fate and Electre becomes the fate of a whole race.[4] Geneviève serves "le destin" and the characters in *Amphitryon 38* live under its laws.[5]

*Judith* is the only play of Giraudoux to which he affixed the name of tragedy, and it is the first play in which one of his heroines becomes apparent as an exile.

The town in which Judith lives is being threatened with destruction by an invading army headed by Holopherne. The high priest of the town claims that Judith can save it: he wants to make her, "une grande Juive, une héroïne: une femme hors de son destin, une déclassée."[6] Judith's uncle and her suitor, Jean, are opposed to the wishes of the priest, to which Judith nevertheless yields. Like Hélène in *La Guerre de Troie n'aura pas lieu*, who does not see the existence of things unless she thinks them important, Judith claims that Holopherne, the barbarian king, does not exist. There are only means of suffering and redemption which have his name.[7] She explains to Suzanne that she has already entrusted this mission to herself, and now that she is the elected of God she will complete it and thereby save her town. Judith is already by the end of the first act, different from other people. She has been chosen to carry out the will of God.

She goes to the camp of Holopherne and speaks to the pederast Egon who impersonates his leader. Judith pleads her case before him while he and the soldiers mock her. Her shock when she discovers that she has been speaking with an impersonator is overpowering, for she believed herself chosen by God, and she has been tricked not only by the soldiers, but by God himself because he has let this happen to her. When the real Holopherne arrives he finds a humble Judith before him. She is pleased to see him and, recognizing him to be the first real *man* she has ever met, falls in love with him. She is charmed by his individuality which is expressed when he claims that he has no need of gods, that he is a man of *this* world and therefore the worst enemy of God. But Judith, in speaking before Egon, has made her gesture and fate has been alerted. She must now carry through her intention of murdering Holopherne. She tells Suzanne:

I know God better than you do. God is concerned with appearances and totalities, not with details. He insists that we dress up our acts to look like sacrifices, but He leaves us free, beneath that ample garment, to satisfy our own desires, even the basest ones. Since He has exhausted my sense of dedication and my hatred against nonentities before putting me face to face with the real Holopherne, he needed my act, not my support.[8]

She has become her destiny and apparently inhuman. Holopherne points out to her that she really loves nobody. Yesterday she loved the world at large; today she detests it in detail, but, like God or le Destin—the terms are interchangeable—she is not interested in details. He continues by informing her that a woman is a being who has found her nature; Judith has not found hers because she is a virgin. Judith replies that it is her nature to search. (She will find her true self when she sleeps with Holopherne.) She spends the night with the barbarian king and murders him not because her people's fate depends upon this act but because she has experienced love and knows that she will never be able to experience it so fully again. Because of this deed she becomes a symbol of murder and hatred to her people; she is a saint. Judith is aware that she is alienated from humanity because God has pursued her and forced her to become his puppet:

Since the day when He chose me, because of my purity, God's look has soiled me. . . . Beneath the cataclysms which arouse races and men by the thousands, He dissimulates his obstinacy at pursuing one human being and making that hunted animal beg for mercy. . . . There are no histories of peoples. There are only histories of God's hunting out some half-intelligent men and some halfway beautiful women.[9]

God has made Judith a murderer; he has soiled her purity, and this is her tragedy.

If pride as well as submission to fatality made Judith go to Holopherne in the first place, this same pride makes her accept being a saint at the conclusion of the play. Judith's switch from the terrestrial to the divine in the last act is not very clear but when the guard tells her that her act was inspired by God and not by love she almost too readily believes him: he has previously said that God had decided that Holopherne would not touch her. She has two choices at this moment, one which we expect her to make—and which she attempts to make—namely, renouncing her act as an act of vengeance and describing it as one of love, one which is essentially anti-divine, and the second to claim that she killed Holopherne because of her hatred of him. The first choice would lead to scorn, complete alienation, and possibly death. The second will lead to exile, but her encounter with Holopherne and his revelations to her have already made her a spiritual exile anyway, and her pride tells her to choose this second way.[10] Judith has lost and God has won; Judith is still a virgin; the better is destroyed by the worse, and this is Judith's tragedy. She becomes a saint who will see no one, who will spend the rest of her life in the temple judging the sins of others.

Isabelle in *Intermezzo* is in rebellion against the hypocritical society in which she lives. She claims that everything which she has been taught is ridiculous, that school learning has nothing to do with the outside world. She finds escape in communing with a ghost which is currently haunting the provincial region in which she lives. The ghost has upset the town; the poorest man has won the lottery instead of the millionaire, and the two oldest people have died instead of young ones. Because Isabelle has been communing with the ghost, the Droguiste is worried. He says, "How touching it is to see innocence revolving thus, without suspicion and without peril, around symbols of evil."[11] He remarks that Isabelle has always been different from her companions, and says that fate has chosen her for the role of communing with the ghost. Because of this choice Isabelle has been alienated from everyday existence. And her disgust with existence in her town increases the more she is attracted by the supernatural as represented by the ghost.

Isabelle teaches a group of little girls, but her instruction is hardly of the type prescribed in French educational circles. This is clearly shown in her first encounter with the Inspecteur, a materialist who supervises education in Isabelle's region. Isabelle tells him that she is making sure that her pupils do not believe in the injustice of nature. The Inspecteur, who has been informed of Isabelle's communing with the ghost, questions the girls about various prescribed subjects and finds them very poorly informed. He is determined to get to the bottom of the problem. The conflict between Isabelle and him is one of the major themes of the play, for each represents an extreme. Isabelle, who is a representative of imagination and poetry, is willing to deny earthly existence while he, who represents the flat conformism of a literal mind, defends human life for the wrong reasons.

When the Contrôleur asks Isabelle what human knowledge is, she replies:

What one calls thus is at most human religion and it is a terrible selfishness. Its dogma is to make impossible or sterile all liaisons with anything not human, to unlearn all the languages that a child already knows, except the human language. In that fraudulent modesty, that stupid obeying of prejudices, what marvelous advances have we not rejected from all the layers of the world and from all kingdoms. I alone dared to answer. My answer to the dead is only the first.[12]

All of the other characters see in this response a negation of life. It is possible for us to see, however, that Isabelle is not negating life but rather embracing an aspect of it of which her fellow citizens seem unaware. She is an idealist who pursues her ideal incessantly. This pursuit upsets the daily routine in her town but she does prove to several people, in any case, that there is something to be desired which is beyond crass materialism and the monotony of existence. Two plans are devised to bring her back to reality. The representatives of earthly poetry, the Contrôleur and the Droguiste, suggest that they try to interest Isabelle in living by forcing her to live with them. The bureaucrats, headed by the Inspecteur, decide that the only way to cure the young girl is to kill the ghost. The latter method fails; but the first is not successful either. The Contrôleur, who sees that Isabelle is quickly becoming permanently alienated from the world of humans, warns her of the power of the other world:

Their game is well known. They apply themselves to separating one person from the human group. They attract him, by pity or curiosity, far from the flock which takes pleasure in dresses and ties, which likes bread and wine, and they absorb him. Your ghost is doing exactly that.[13]

He tries to convince her of the danger in touching the extremes of existence. Life, he goes on, is full between the two extremes. If she insists upon touching one she will become permanently alienated and there will be repercussions in the whole social structure.

Isabelle remains entranced by the ghost, however, who tells her that he will appear in her room the next day. Just before the ghost is to arrive the Contrôleur enters and asks Isabelle to marry him. He pleads his cause and the cause of earthly existence with such fervor and beauty that Isabelle seems almost persuaded. The ghost then appears and engages the Contrôleur in a verbal duel. The Spectre says that as young girls mature they are attracted by the absolute; they want to understand the secrets of life and death. However, a man invariably appears and snatches them away from this world of inquiry, and the young girls fall in love. The ghost renounces trying to convince Isabelle because the Contrôleur has made his plea; he is the man to break the spell which has been cast over the young girl:

Goodbye, Isabelle. Your Contrôleur is right. What men love, what you love, is not acquaintance or knowledge but rather oscillating between two truths or two lies, between Gap and Bressuire.[14]

Isabelle tries to keep the ghost from disappearing but, failing to do so, faints. To revive her the Droguiste decides that life must go on around her. Everyone must perform his customary tasks, and as they do so Isabelle slowly revives. She is cured; no longer is she an exile. It has taken a pronouncement from the other world to break her implacable will and make her conform to life, just as the angel in *Judith* convinced the heroine that she must become a saint. There is an interesting parallel between Judith and Isabelle. Judith meets Holopherne, learns from him what magnificence the world contains, and falls in love with him. God and destiny mean little to her until her pride is given consistency by the angel. Isabelle meets the Contrôleur and learns from him what it is to enjoy the world without being in communion with the dead. But whereas Judith's sainthood accentuates her previous exile, Isabelle's marriage will make her a part of society again.

The Contrôleur recognizes the fact that if Isabelle sees ghosts she also sees the living as they are, and that she is the only one who does so. She sees things as they are and only the things which are important to her really exist. One can see in her the currents of life because her intimate liaison with the world's phenomena makes her more aware of reality itself.[15] This is the most distinguishing characteristic of Giraudoux's women.

If Isabelle tries to escape from everyday existence, which she cannot tolerate because of its hypocrisy, Electre tries to see and understand her own existence. She is just as implacable in her search as Isabelle is in her evasion.

Electre is a seeker of truth and nothing turns her from it. Of all Giraudoux's heroines she is the most clearly defined as an exile. Before she sets foot on stage we have heard her called "une femme à histoires" by the Président. He says that she is dangerous to the state because she embodies elements fatal to humanity:

I know Electre. Let's agree that she is what you say—justice, generosity, duty. But it's by justice, generosity, duty, and not by egoism and easy-going ways, that the state, individuals, and the best families are ruined. . . . Because these three virtues have in common the one element fatal to humanity—implacability. Happiness is never the lot of implacable people. A happy family makes a surrender. A happy epoch demands unanimous capitulation.[16]

Electre, he continues, makes the sins which he committed in the cradle stir in his mind: she is integral justice. (The very vulgarity which Electre detests is personified by the Président and his wife, Agathe. Capitulation to mediocrity, satisfaction with one's vulgar condition are what Electre will eventually battle against when she declares herself.)

Egisthe agrees with the Président's opinion of Electre but finds it too bourgeois. He proceeds to define his conception of fate, telling how he has waged merciless war on those who could possibly signal to the Gods. He feels that it is the chief duty of a head of a state:

If for ten years the gods have not meddled with our lives, it's because I've kept the heights empty and the fairgrounds full. I've ordered dreamers, painters, and chemists to marry; and because, in order to avoid racial trouble between our citizens—something that can't help marking human beings as different in the eyes of the gods—I've always given great importance to misdemeanors and paid slight attention to crimes.[17]

Because Egisthe has disposed of the painters, dreamers, and chemists who give meaning to life, there is only one person in Argos who can signal to the Gods and that person is Electre. He has attempted to cope with Electre by affiancing her to the Jardinier, hoping thereby to keep her from causing destruction. The Mendiant, who serves as a sort of chorus, poses the question—will the king declare himself in Egisthe before Electre declares herself in Electre. Electre declares herself first.

Electre has one characteristic in common with Sartre's Oreste, and it is this characteristic that brings about a revolution in both *Les Mouches* and *Electre*. Neither she nor Oreste ever gives a second thought to the fact that he or she might be wrong. Both are completely convinced of the justification of their acts. Clytemnestre makes this quite clear when she asks, "How does it happen that she doesn't understand that even in good faith she can be wrong?"[18]

By the end of the first act Electre is well on the way to the knowledge of her truth. Even before she has discovered the truth about the murder of her father and her mother's attachment to Egisthe, she becomes, the Mendiant tells us, ". . . unadulterated truth, a lamp without a wick."[19] She will accomplish her destiny because she is now on the trail of truth:

. . . for the young girl is the guardian of truth; she has to go after it whether or not the world bursts and cracks down to its foundations, whether innocents die the death of innocents, to let the guilty live their guilty lives.[20]

Like Isabelle, Electre has the effect on people of making them tell the truth. Everyone does but Clytemnestre and the Mendiant, and even in Clytemnestre the truth will out: it is as strong as Electre says it is. She says to her daughter, "All the evil in the world came from so-called pure people wanting to unearth secrets and airing them."[21] Then through the intermediary of Agathe and her husband Electre discovers that Clytemnestre has been the mistress of Egisthe and that together they murdered Agamemnon. She damns the gods.

I don't doubt it. I recognize in it the hyprocrisy and malice of the gods. They change a parasite into a just man, an adulterer into a husband, a usurper into a king. They thought my task not painful enough, so they made a figure of honor out of you, whom I despise! But there's one change they can't carry through! They can't transform a criminal into an innocent man. They bow to me there.[22]

Electre is implacable. She is going to see justice done, and even though she knows that Egisthe alone is capable of saving Argos from the attacking Corinthian armies she declares that her duty is the enemy of the duty of Egisthe. Justice must be accomplished at all cost, and Electre will not permit the marriage of her mother to the usurper of her father's throne. When Egisthe asks her whether her justice consists of rendering all acts irreparable she replies, "No! . . . But when a crime threatens human dignity, infects a race, rots its loyalty, there is no pardon."[23] She makes Oreste kill Egisthe and Clytemnestre. Justice has been done.

Because of Electre's search for truth and justice she is an exile who is looked upon with fear and suspicion. She accomplishes her destiny without regard for the consequences. She makes Oreste commit the murders and then does not hesitate to sacrifice him on the altar of truth.[24] She sacrifices her country for the sake of a truth and still feels a great innocence and sense of liberty. Yet she is as much an exile at the play's conclusion as she was at its opening. She has no family left; Oreste has gone mad; her country is in enemy hands. The last few speeches are indicative of her status:

Electre:    I have my conscience, I have Orestes, I have justice, I have everything.

Second Fury: Your conscience! Will you listen to your conscience in the early mornings to come? For seven years you've not slept because of a crime that others committed. Now you're the guilty one.

Electre:    I have Orestes, I have justice, I have everything.

Third Fury:  Orestes! You'll never see Orestes again. We're leaving *you*—to pursue *him*. We've taken on your age and shape—to pursue him. Good-bye! We'll not leave him until he's been driven to madness or suicide, cursing his sister.

Electre:    I have justice. I have everything.[25]

Justice is all she is left with at the end of the play, justice and an ironic dawn. In speaking of this Sorensen says: "Everything risks being lost, but the conclusion remains still optimistic: a new hope grows out of the ruins of falsehood."[26]

With most of Giraudoux's other critics Sorensen seems convinced that not only is this play but most of the others concluded on an optimistic note. This interpretation seems fallacious. *Electre* ends on an ironic note. The Eumenides have shown the sister of Oreste that she has nothing but her justice, but of what use is justice if thousands of innocent people die to attain it? Giraudoux was too much of a humanist to believe that the end justifies the means. Electre's tragic flaw is her very search for justice: this is what distinguishes her from others. And she has nothing but her justice at the end of the play. If the conclusion of the play is optimistic why does the following dialogue ensue between the Femme Narsès and the Mendiant? (Oreste has just entered after committing the murders.)

La Femme Narsès: There is the young man! How beautiful he is!
Le Mendiant:      As beautiful as the young Aegisthus.[27]

The story is about to repeat itself. There is just another murder to atone for, and the cycle begins again. This can hardly be called optimistic; at best it is an attitude of resignation. The last line of the play can only be explained in this manner. The Mendiant says ironically, "That is called the dawn."[28] In other words man can only be purified through wholesale destruction. Optimistic?

In many of Giraudoux's plays the story repeats itself at the conclusion. Ondine, viewing the body of the dead Hans, says, "How I would have loved him!"[29] The Inspecteur of *Intermezzo* says, "The case of Isabelle is closed. The case of Luce will crop up only in three or four years."[30] The Angel says at the close of *Sodome et Gomorrhe*, "Death has not sufficed. The scene continues."[31] Optimistic? I should hardly call them so.[32]

Electre is the heroine who most clearly poses the major problem with which Giraudoux is concerned. She presents man's potentialities as opposed to Clytemnestre who symbolizes man's mediocrity. The reality of existence as seen in *Electre* is as horrible as that of the Paris of *La Folle de Chaillot* or of Sodom. To cleanse the world of its imperfections and make the essences such as justice, beauty, honor which in Giraudoux's thought, as in Plato's, precede the existences, triumph, wholesale slaughter must be invoked. Giraudoux seems to have believed that not only has man lost Eden but that he has also lost any awareness of what Eden might have been like, so deluded is he by years of superstition and crime. Wholesale destruction of human beings by his heroines is therefore resorted to in his theatre. These heroines have a vision of Eden, and as long as they exist there is still some hope for man. Yet Giraudoux is paradoxical. The pessimism which becomes apparent at the conclusion of each play seems to contradict that hope.

Electre represents integral justice and through her and her actions life is given meaning because justice and nobility of spirit triumph. Yet she does not seem to be a tragic figure, because she is too much above the battle. She is, in distinction from Sartre's heroes, terrifyingly calm in the moment of crisis. She cannot compromise with Égisthe when he asks for respite in order to put down the Corinthian invaders because the slightest defection from her course will defeat the cause of justice. Essence, which in this play is integral justice, is so much more important than existence to Electre that the latter loses much of its meaning. Electre's seeming unawareness of existence takes from her the tragic stature which she might otherwise have had. She therefore becomes an abstraction whose one-sided awareness of the universe makes her in no wise pathetic.

Ondine is a water sprite who tries to become a woman because she loves a man. The king of the Ondins says of her:

If someone didn't give a rap about human secrets it is she. Evidently men have treasures: gold, jewels; but what she preferred was their most commonplace objects, her stool, her spoon. . . . She is the most human woman there has ever been precisely because she was so by choice.[33]

Someone who speaks a language too perfectly can almost invariably be detected as a foreigner, and so Ondine who is too perfect a woman can be detected as an outsider, someone who has not been reared to be a woman.

Almost all of Ondine's problems arise from the fact that not having been brought up as a human being she cannot understand their ways, their hypocrisies, their infidelities. Because of this she is always an alien looking in on a world which she cannot understand or else understands too well and is not able to accept.

A young chevalier, Hans von Wittenstein zu Wittenstein, appears one night at the cottage of Auguste, a fisherman who lives at the side of a lake with his wife, Eugénie. Ondine, their adopted daughter, sees Hans and falls in love with him. She says, "I knew well there had to be a reason to be a girl. The reason is that men are so handsome."[34] He succumbs to her charm and makes her his wife. Ondine, who has, however, been warned by the king of the Ondins to avoid men because they are deceitful, has her own ideas. She makes a pact with the king of the Ondins, however. She promises that if Hans is unfaithful to her before she is unfaithful to him he will be killed and she will return to the kingdom of the Ondins and lose her memory.

The king of the Ondins represents fate, the supernatural force which pervades all of Giraudoux's plays and provides the essential conflict within them. Ondine has alerted this force by marrying Hans and it only awaits his infidelity to strike. Auguste warns of this force in the first act. His *nature* is strangely akin to the *destin* of the Greek plays or the *Dieu* of the Biblical ones:

It is true that nature doesn't like to become angry at man. It is prejudiced in his favor. Something in him wins it over or amuses it. All the venom and poison in flowers and reptiles flees, at the approach of man, towards shadows or betrays itself by its very color. But if man has once offended nature he is lost.[35]

Auguste tells Hans that Ondine is nature itself:

It is either because children guess instinctively what nature is, or it is because the nature of Ondine is nature itself. There are great forces about Ondine.[36]

These forces, once unleashed, provide the tragic climax of the play and Ondine, because of her very perfection, is really the force which is her own undoing.[37]

The first symptom of exile, apart from the already mentioned birth and rearing of Ondine, comes at the end of the first act. She tells Hans that sea dogs live together for life and asks him whether the king and queen in his country live as closely. Hans replies that it would be difficult for them to do so because each has his own apartments, his own means of transportation, his own gardens. Ondine comments, "What a frightening word is each." For the first time she realizes that she is different and that her ideas do not coincide with those of man. She is integral purity, a virtue denied most women.

The Illusioniste in the second act is the king of the Ondins, who has disguised himself. He represents *le destin* which has been described in *La Guerre de Troie n'aura pas lieu* as "la forme accélérée du temps." Here he accelerates time and we see Hans falling in love with Bertha. Ondine is quite obviously out of place at court and when she realizes that Hans has betrayed her has a verbal duel with Bertha. The queen, Yseult, takes her aside and speaks with her, and this scene, perhaps more than any other, emphasizes Ondine's alienation. Yseult tells Ondine that what the sprite is seeking is a man who will be hers alone rather than one who exists separately as well as with her and that this type of man is very rare.[38] The queen sees that Ondine is different because, like the other heroines of Giraudoux, she has a thirst for the infinite, and, at the same time, she is transparent:

Yseult:   Whether you seek truth or falsehood, dear child, you will deceive no one and you will offer men what they detest most.
Ondine:  Faithfulness?
Yseult:   No, transparency. They are afraid of it. To them it seems the worst secret. When Hans sees that you are not a residue of memories, a mass of projects, a stockpile of impressions and wishes, he will be afraid and you will be lost.[39]

Ondine, like most of Giraudoux's women, is transparent. She is a sort of mirror faithful to the deep currents of the world, and by herself she is nothing at all.[40]

Ondine realizes that Hans has betrayed her. But she also realizes that this means his death because in her world there is no pardon, and it is by her world that he has been condemned. Her world is very much like that of Electre, and Electre in many respects is similar to the king of the Ondins.[41] Ondine speaks of her world and compares it to the world of humanity:

Mankind, as you call it, is quite tiny in the universe. Mankind which forgets, changes its mind, pardons. In our world as in the world of wild beasts, ash-tree leaves, caterpillars, there is no renouncing or pardon.[42]

She tries to deceive the king of the Ondins by saying she betrayed Hans first, but her ruses fail. Hans dies and she returns to her sisters.

There is more humanity about Ondine than about most of the Giraudoux heroines, perhaps because, as her uncle the king of the Ondins explains it, she was not born a woman; she was a woman by choice. Yet her very humanity exiles her from the society of man. She tries to save Hans from death and fails. She is not implacable like Judith or Electre. They have little chance to compromise with their destiny because they are it. But Ondine struggles with her destiny, and, even though she knows it is fruitless, fights for the life of her beloved.

Lia, the heroine of *Sodome et Gomorrhe*, resembles the other heroines of Giraudoux in her search for truth, but the truth which she is seeking is one of the most elusive, the secret of the stable and happy marriage. Lia's case is even more pathetic than Judith's or Electre's because she is a spiritual exile from life for almost purely physical and psychological reasons.[43] Like Judith, Lia wants a man, not a counterfeit, but she never finds him whereas Judith did find Holopherne. Like Isabelle she is in touch with the supernatural, the supernatural in her case being an angel. Like Electre she desires truth at all costs. But unlike Electre and more reminiscent of Ondine, Lia has a human quality about her which makes her an almost likable character.

*Sodome et Gomorrhe* is a pessimistic play about the inability of the sexes to find any kind of permanent relationship. Both the men and the women have their grievances against the other and neither will compromise, and thus they are all destroyed by God.

Lia's grievances against Jean, her husband, are perhaps all contained in the fact that she can never possess him completely. Like Ondine, and undoubtedly like an older Isabelle, she can achieve her happiness only through perfect fusion. This may also explain why Judith killed Holopherne. Having experienced total fusion with him she realized it could not last, and, rather than fall into a predicament like Lia's, she killed him to avoid disillusion.

Lia says that Jean has changed since their marriage:

All charms are fastened on the man you marry. He is an elm laden with finches who welcome you. Then, week by week, each finch flies off on another man, and at the end of the year your husband is disseminated on all the others.[44]

In reality, Jean has not changed. The optics of his wife have changed. Lia tires of Jean, and Jean, wounded in his most vulnerable spot, his pride, begins to lose interest in Lia. Lia's frankness in telling Jean that he bores her is what has caused the profound upheaval in their marriage. If she had said nothing Jean would not have noticed that his marriage was falling apart. Lia is a true Giraudoux heroine, however, and therefore speaks the truth.

Lia claims that men's bodies are their alibis. They can dissimulate their essential absence only through their bodies. She wants Jean's body to speak to her, to be completely hers. She says, "Your body is turned away, silent. O Jean, when will you speak?"[45]

If Lia is exiled from man because of her frankness and his unwillingness to give completely of himself, she is also exiled from God, and she realizes it, because God is a man. She believes that all evil comes from God because he is a man,[46] and she therefore feels alienated from him.

Lia's interest turns from Jean to Jacques, but after her experiences with the latter she realizes that total fusion is impossible with any man. This is why she turns to the Angel. Her happiness is in the realm of the impossible. When the Angel says, "Your concern is yourself. Life is your life,"[47] he indicates Lia's major problem. She, like the other Giraudoux heroines, is essentially an egoist.

As with Electre, Lia's very passion for truth alienates her from others; it acts on Jean the way the exceptional qualities of Electre act on the Président and Egisthe, who falls in love with her. Jean says,

You are what I admire most in the world, Lia, and from that only discouragement is born in me. You are what I believe, what I know as the truth, generosity, and they act on me only as duplicity and selfishness would act. You are what I love most in the world and your love inspires in me only what the disgust of another would inspire.[48]

After her failure to win the Angel, Lia tries to return to Jean but she finds living with him impossible. She cannot be hypocritical even though man can. She cries to God that if he wants man to be happy he must create an adult man, and, realizing the impossibility of happiness, she awaits the end of the world. Lia will not compromise, and although this makes her admirable, her awareness of *la condition humaine* is not nearly as powerful as her awareness of her ideal and she therefore loses the pathetic quality common to classic heroes.

Jean sees another characteristic of Lia which also belongs to the other Giraudoux heroines. He claims that in searching for truth she is tearing off man's mask when actually she is ripping off his face. This unawareness of the reality of Life's appearance and the consequent searching for something super-human is not only a fault of Giraudoux's women but a condemnation of them as tragic creations. Lia says as much herself when she tells Jean: "God let an Angel talk. He had Satan. Man let his wife talk. He had woman."[49] And because woman has spoken too frankly there can be no happy marriage except in outward appearance. God therefore destroys Sodome and Gommorhe.

The heroines of Giraudoux have as much admirable about them as any other characters in modern drama. They defend ideals, poetry, justice, beauty; in short, the finer things in the universe, from the mediocrity and baseness of the world as Giraudoux sees it. The absolutes which they embody, when exemplified and defended, can give meaning to life, can justify existence as they often do in the classical drama. But the exile-heroines of Giraudoux seem in the long run to lack the tragic stature of an Antigone, a Lear, or a Phèdre precisely because the ideals which they embody become abstractions which, while appearing to demonstrate a theory, seem more important than existence itself. In the classical drama most of the heroes seem to experience some moment of doubt. They wonder, for example, whether the state or some ideal is more important than themselves and their own happiness, and this moment of doubt makes them more human than they might otherwise seem. This human attitude of doubt is invariably missing in Giraudoux's women.

The heroines of Giraudoux are as egotistical as many other characters in the modern drama. They are always convinced of the justification for their actions, and there are few, if any, instances of doubt in their minds in the course of the action of any particular play. We admire them for their tenacity in pursuing and embodying their absolute, but their apparent unawareness or unconcern for the state, or better still, existence, makes the balance unequal. The world, *la condition humaine*, is not an adversary worthy of them. As in Anouilh's theatre, it is portrayed in the blackest colors and the irony and pessimism of Giraudoux only serve to underline this blackness. When at the end of each play someone says, in one way or another, "La scène continue" we wonder whether the proofs these heroines have offered us of man's occasional majesty are tenable. Giraudoux is so ironic that it is often difficult to ascertain his position, although, if we judge from the plays, we may be sure that he is pessimistic about the future of man. What his heroine-exiles have done is point up the vulgar aspects of man without either justifying his existence or offering any proof that their great personal sacrifices have not been made in vain. As such Giraudoux's plays fail to become tragedy. They tend to become attacks on contemporary society, which Giraudoux, always with an ironic and impenetrable smile, seems to condemn. And his heroines consequently appear to be abstractions, charming and admirable ones, to be sure, who are spokesmen for, or ideals of, their creator rather than perfectly credible tragic figures.

## CHAPTER VI

# The Existentialist And The Absurd Man

WE feel a strange affinity with the heroes of Sartre doubtless because they have many admirable character traits. And thus we often find ourselves substituting ourselves rather than our neighbors for them as we observe the plays. The exile of Sartre is the person who often comes closest to being a tragic figure in the modern French theatre. I do not mean to imply by this statement that Sartre's plays are necessarily better than those of any other contemporary French dramatist or that his characters are more memorable. They are not. There is, however, something genuinely pathetic and admirable about the heroes of at least five of his plays which makes us more aware of ourselves and of man's fate in general.

Sartre's heroes, as differentiated from most others in the modern drama, are not primarily unhealthy people and, although they have problems which are essentially their own, they can be said to be representative of active twentieth-century men. They are all aware of their times, and they are usually a part of them. They all have objectives and, bizarre enough in the modern theatre, many of them do actually accomplish the task which they have set for themselves. Oreste in *Les Mouches* frees Argos from its remorse. Goetz in *Le Diable et le bon Dieu* finds both himself and a personal meaning in life, even though he is a broken man. The Maquisards, although ironically shot at the close of *Morts sans sépultures*, discover that their battle against the Nazis has not been lost. Hugo of *Les Mains sales* walks into death not through a sense of false heroics but because his death will give meaning to the death of Hoederer; he has balanced his account with society. It is only *Huis-Clos* and *La Putain respectueuse* which end pessimistically with the ways of man still unjustified.

Each of the heroes of Sartre has an overwhelming feeling of loneliness, of alienation from his fellow man, but this sense of alienation does not nullify his participation in the affairs of his society. In fact, it seems that only the exiles in Sartre's plays are able to accomplish anything for the society of which they often wish they were an integral part. The Sartrian hero has a sense of social responsibility which outweighs his hatred of the gods or man. He is born to accomplish something—his act—and to be worthy in his own eyes he must perform it. In *Les Mouches* Oreste's act is to kill his stepfather, Egisthe, and his mother, Clytemnestre, and thereby free the people of Argos from their guilt and remorse.

The first act gives the background of the play, introduces the characters, and sets the stage for the tragic development, the pace of which quickens considerably as the act progresses. Practically the first words uttered by Oreste demonstrate the theme which will continue to be developed throughout the act, the fact that he does not belong in Argos. He tells the Pédagogue that he was born here in Argos and yet must ask his way as a stranger. He is an outsider, an intellectual who has studied the ways of man, who now finds himself in a place where he does not belong. As Eric Bentley points out,[1] he is at this point very much above the battle, his whole attitude being suggested by the line "et quelle superbe absence que mon âme."[2] He is free of all entanglements and, as the Pédagogue tells him, a superior man. Oreste realizes his own superiority but he wants to belong to the people of Argos, to be one of them. When Jupiter tells him that the citizens of Argos are great sinners whose remorse Oreste will never be able to share because he did not share in their crime, Oreste almost involuntarily revolts. He speaks proudly of *his* palace, the palace where he was born and where his father was killed. He already *is* a part of the town, and his attitude varies throughout the first act between his feeling that he would like to belong and the impression that somehow he does belong. The latter is only hinted at, but it is there all the same, as Electre will make clear when she tells her brother that he is of the house of Atreus and, like her, has crime and misfortune in his blood. Oreste's predominant feeling throughout the act, however, is an intense desire to be a part of something, to have something of his own:

Ah! a dog, an old dog who warms himself, lying near the hall and who raises himself a little at the entrance of his master, growling gently to greet him, a dog has more memory than I. It is *his* master whom he recognizes. His master. And what is mine?[3]

He is free and he regrets it, almost bitterly:

There are men who are born *engagés*: they have no choice; they have been thrown on a road at the end of which there is an act awaiting them, *their* act. . . . And there are others, silent ones, who feel at the bottom of their hearts the weight of troubled and earthly images; their life has been changed because one day in their childhood, at five years, at seven years. . . . That's all right: they are not superior men. I knew already, at seven years, that I was exiled. . . . But I . . . I am free.[4]

If he had spent all his life in Argos, if he had seen the children of its citizens born and married, if he had the same memories as they, he would be happy. Actually, so far, and only with subtle hints from Jupiter and occasional remarks from the Pédagogue, Oreste has been convincing himself of his alienation.

It is not until Electre asks him, "But you who come to claim the name of the family of Atreus, who are you to say you are one of us. Have you spent your life in the shadow of a murder?"[5] that Oreste's situation becomes plain to him. He becomes desperate, and sees that in order to become part of the town, in order to belong to Electre, he will have to commit himself by murdering his stepfather and his mother. (We are now well into the second act, and he is still an exile in fact. He will not become a figurative exile until after the murders.) He kills them and in so doing takes upon himself the crimes of the city and the repentance of the citizens. But now he is even more alienated than he was before he committed the murders. Before he could not share the remorse and sense of guilt of the citizens of Argos; now they cannot share *his* crime. He is happy, however, because having committed this act, *his* act, he has something of his own. He says: "I have committed my act, Electre, and that act was good. I shall bear it on my shoulders. . . . And the heavier it is to carry, the more I shall rejoice, for it is my liberty."[6]

Oreste realizes that his new state is one of exile, and he

is proud of it because, by choosing it himself, he has discharged his obligations to his people, and although he is now technically a part of Argos,[7] he refuses the throne, saying he wishes to be a king without a country and without subjects.

Actually what Oreste has done in *Les Mouches* is to challenge the accepted order, religious and political. He has overthrown it by violence, and a new age has begun. This has been imminent throughout the play, because Jupiter and Egisthe both realize and have said that once man discovers their secret—that man is free—they will lose their power. Oreste has understood from the moment he stepped on stage that he is free. He is his own liberty and therefore belongs to no one, and Jupiter, who might in his youth have been another Oreste, sees the approaching twilight of the gods. Jupiter is powerless against Oreste. He says that once liberty has exploded in the mind of a man the gods have no power over him. Only other men, and they alone, can strangle him or let him go on. (Why Jupiter cannot incite or force other men to do this is a point which Sartre seems to have overlooked.) Oreste remarks to Jupiter that he and the god are similar. Could not this suggest that an older Oreste might become another Jupiter? "You are a god and I am free: we are similarly alone and our anguish is similar."[8] The difference between the two lies in the fact that Oreste loves men and wants to aid them whereas Jupiter dislikes them. Oreste has said that in order to love or hate one has to give of one's self. He is capable of this; Jupiter and Egisthe are not.

Oreste might be called a Christ-like figure, although it is doubtful whether Sartre had this in mind when he wrote *Les Mouches*. The young prince is the innocent man who takes upon himself the sins of a guilty city, and, having done this, leaves. Like Christ, also alienated from his world while he lived, Oreste symbolically restores man's dignity. Oreste, like Christ, like any prophet, knows or is assured that what he does is just. He is implacable in his actions. They are his and therefore they are good, and what is good for him is consequently good for other men. When Christ died, He left men with hope rather than despair. Oreste does much the same thing. He has acted and will let men judge him accordingly. However, if Oreste is in some respects a Christ-like figure, he differs from Christ in that he enacts a revolution through violence, whereas Christ's revolution was to be effected through love.

One is reminded of Lenormand's theory of evil when Electre tells Oreste that it is by violence alone that people are cured, and then one wonders whether Sartre is as optimistic as one might have thought at first. Does one evil engender another? Will Oreste's crime be the crime to end all crimes, or is it just a link in an endless chain? Sartre leaves the question unanswered. It might be significant to note, however, that when Oreste leaves he takes the Furies with him.

Electre presents an interesting contrast with her brother. Like Oreste she is alone at the beginning of the play, not because she has to be, but because she has chosen to be. The crime of Egisthe and Clytemnestre is not her crime, and she refuses to atone for it. Yet she feels she belongs in Argos and refuses to flee with Oreste when he asks her to join him. After the murder she is still alone. Her hatred dies when Egisthe is killed, but she becomes exactly what her mother was (as Clytemnestre had told her she would) full of remorse and weighted by her own chains. Whereas Oreste finds his true freedom in the murders, Electre finds only slavery and guilt. Her decision to devote her life to expiation—for she is not strong enough to accept the consequences of her crime and to begin a new life—denies her tragic stature.

If *Les Mouches* shows us redemption, Sartre's second play, *Huis-Clos*, shows us damnation. Oreste accomplishes what he set out to do. The characters of *Huis-Clos* are failures who have been damned to hell. If Oreste has been justified by his *act*, Garcin has been damned because he did not have the courage of his convictions. When Garcin tells Inès that he did not have the time while alive to perform his acts, she informs him that one always dies too soon or too late, that one is necessarily bound by the limits of one's own life. And the mood of the play is, therefore, that of an elegy on lives gone astray, rather than that of tragedy which justifies man.

Hell in *Huis-Clos* consists of an Empire drawing room without mirrors or windows. In it have been put, not by chance, but by an almost too careful predestination, Inès, a Lesbian who was a post office clerk; Garcin, a coward who was shot by his government after trying to flee his South American country to avoid military service; and Estelle, a superficial café society girl who has committed infanticide. Inès, a Fearon of more refined perversity, a perversity which probably results from her introversion, was already damned on earth, alienated from her society because of her Lesbianism. Her great loneliness comes from the fact that because she enjoys their suffering she needs others to exist. Estelle, who seldom thought and merely enjoyed herself, has always been extroverted. The misfortunes of others, such as the suicide of the young man who loved her, left her unmoved. She was, and is, a vain woman interested only in her own pleasure. Garcin, who, as Bentley points out,[9] seems the least guilty of the three, is a coward who lacked the courage essential to become a hero. And throughout the play he tries in vain to convince the others (and himself) that he was not a coward.

These three are damned to spend eternity together, and it is only as the play progresses that we see how horrible their fate is. There is no human dignity in hell. Each is stripped of it before the other two; each is apart because of his past life. Inès' Lesbianism and Garcin's coarse language terrify and shock Estelle. Garcin can have no sexual bonds with Inès and no mental bonds with Estelle. Attempts are made throughout the play by each of these characters to nullify his isolation, but these do not succeed. Inès tries unsuccessfully to seduce Estelle. Estelle tries to seduce Garcin, but Inès, by her very presence, thwarts Estelle's attempt.

Disgusted with Estelle's superficiality and Inès' taunts, Garcin decides he will leave the room, but when the door opens none of the three has the courage to depart. Each realizes that he is better off where he is than somewhere else. At the end of the play all three laugh hysterically. They realize, as Garcin says, that hell is other people. Each is irremediably alone with himself, and, at the same time, alone with others present. Hell is complete alienation and yet, paradoxically, it is intolerable because of the presence of others.

The optimistic note is again struck in Sartre's next play, *Morts sans sépultures*. A group of French Maquisards, captured by the Vichy French, are in an attic waiting to be questioned and tortured by their captors. Each of them is in a different situation. Canoris, the Greek, now middle-aged, has been tortured before and is hardened to life. Sorbier, a young man, is not afraid of death but dreads physical suffering. Henri, a young medical student, loves Lucie, another of the captives, who in turn, loves and is the mistress of Jean, the leader of their group. Lucie's young brother, François, a fourteen-year-old, desires to live at any cost.

Each is alone with his thoughts and each feels his own

solitude while awaiting his turn to be questioned. Each feels guilty because others have lost their lives through his Resistance activities. The beginning of the play is shrouded in the deepest pessimism because each character is in a state of doubt, discomfort, and anguish. Henri might be speaking for all five when he says, "It's with myself alone that I must reckon at present."[10] Canoris carries the pessimistic mood a bit further, claiming that all of them are already dead; they died when they ceased to be useful. Henri continues his introspective thoughts, which do little to raise the morale of the group:

At present no one can give me more orders and nothing can justify me any more. A bit of life in excess. Yes, just the time I need to concentrate on my own problems.[11]

Then, in a tone which is quite reminiscent of Garcin, he comments that all of them have been unable to justify their lives. Now they are going to die unjustifiable deaths.

With the arrival of Jean, whose identity is not known to the police who have captured him, their spirits improve for, as Henri says, Jean's appearance has given them a reason for dying. They will die knowing that he is safe and carrying on their work:

Listen! If you had not come we would have suffered like animals, without knowing why. But you are here, and all that is going to happen now will have meaning. . . . I believed I was completely useless, but I see now that there is something for which I am necessary. With a little luck, I could perhaps tell myself that my death is not meaningless.[12]

As Canoris, Henri, and Lucie are tortured (Sorbier has already committed suicide) the symbol of exile changes. Whereas before, Lucie, Henri, and Canoris felt themselves to be alone, they now have their common suffering to hold them together, and Jean becomes the outsider who cannot join their suffering. In this respect he is much like Oreste who, upon his arrival in Argos, could not share the remorse of the town. Oreste, however, commits an act which permits him to acquire the guilt of everyone. Jean can do nothing. He cannot join his friends in their suffering because they are now of a different world, one which he cannot know because he feels more than they his responsibility to other people. He must continue in the Resistance.

Because François has threatened to tell his captors what they want to know, Canoris and Henri strangle him. The fact that Jean is horrified by this act alienates him even more from the group. When Lucie, whom he loves, gives way to false heroics the gulf that has sprung up between them widens still further. Jean is disgusted, but there is nothing he can do, because they have undergone something that he has not and he therefore is not one of them.

When their captors offer them freedom in return for information about Jean, Lucie and Henri want to refuse. They both desire death. Henri, filled with remorse at having killed François, wants to be sure he did not kill the youth through pride.[13] But he will never know. The force of Jean's question—whether suffering was necessary for a clear conscience—returns to him when he realizes he may have been wrong in killing François. And death appears to be the only escape from his doubts.

Lucie wants to die because she wants to be a heroine. In fact, having submitted to torture, she already feels herself to be one. Death would put the finishing touch on her portrait as a martyr. Eric Bentley, commenting on the psychology of heroism, says that Lucie is descending to heroics:

The psychology of heroism is complex. The hero is prepared to die for the cause if necessary. But if he wishes to die when it is *not* necessary, when indeed his life might well be of more use than his death, he is not rising to heroism but descending to heroics.[14]

Canoris believes that they should give the false information and live, and tries to convince Henri that even if he did kill François through pride he can still live and hold his head up. He tells him that his life will be judged by all his acts, and that nothing will be more absurd than his death if he can still work for the Resistance. Lucie and Henri are convinced by the argument of Canoris and decide to reveal the false information. They do so, but ironically one of their captors orders them shot. They die as heroes.

*Morts sans sépultures* might easily be described as a play about heroes and heroics. This is certainly one of its dominant themes. François shouts throughout the first act that he does not want to die, that he is not a hero and that he does not want to be a martyr. His sister, Lucie, does want to be a heroine and gives way to heroics, mistaking them for true heroism. Sorbier is neither a coward nor a hero. His suicide is an act of affirmation and one of negation at the same time. He affirms by his death that what he fought for was good and that he is willing to protect it, for, by committing suicide, he is combatting his own fear of revealing information under torture. It is a negative act because suicide is always negative. Henri is too much like Garcin to be a hero and yet his strangling of François is in some respects reminiscent of Oreste's killing of Egisthe and Clytemnestre. In killing François he is affirming his own belief in his cause, thereby saving the lives of sixty Maquisards. The real heroes of the play are, however, Jean, who will continue working for the Resistance, and Canoris, who will stoop to subterfuge in order to carry on the work of his group. Unfortunately, neither of the two really attains the stature of a tragic hero because the emphasis of the play is divided too equally among the four leading characters. There is no central character, nor any sharp focus by the playwright on any one individual. At the end we are left with the impression of group heroism rather than of a tragic hero.

*La Putain respectueuse* need not concern us long. The play is a complete failure in which the characterizations are mere caricatures and the plot of which is the sheerest melodrama. It seems incredible that the play should have appealed to the French, and even more incredible that they should have believed its content to be true. Sartre shows no insight whatsoever into American social customs, and the play, because of this and the poor characterizations, rings false. Two characters in the play, however, are alienated from the society in which they live—Lizzie, the prostitute, and the Negro. If Sartre wished to portray man's fate by underlining the alienation of Lizzie and the Negro, he failed signally.

Hugo in *Les Mains sales* is, like Oreste and Jean, alienated from the social group. Like Oreste, he has been set apart by his background from the people with whom he is working—the members of the communist party in a middle European country. He is a wealthy bourgeois whereas his co-workers are from the working class. They taunt him with his background so often that he cries desperately from time to time, "No, I have never gone hungry. Never! Never! Never!"[15] Hugo explains his feeling of alienation in speaking of Slick

and Georges, two hirelings who delight in taunting him because of his wealthy upbringing:

> . . . they came to make me pay for my father and my grandfather
> and all those of my family who ate while they went hungry. I
> tell you I know them. They will never accept me. . . . I have
> struggled, I have humiliated myself, I have done everything to
> make them forget. I have repeated to them that I liked them,
> that I envied them, that I admired them. Nothing does any good.
> I am a rich man's son, an intellectual, one who does not work
> with his hands.[16]

Hugo often seems to be a combination of all the previous
Sartre heroes. He has Oreste's dedication to the task that is to
be done although not his compulsion to see it through. He has
a trace of Garcin's cowardice, much of Henri's self-probing.
When he tells us that he is not a coward but not courageous
either we immediately think of Garcin and Henri.

Hugo is alone throughout the play. Even his wife, Jessica,
is outside his sphere. He tells her that her advice comes from
another world; it would have been better had he not asked her
for assistance in his plan to kill Hoederer. Hoederer emphasizes Hugo's difference when he tells him:

> How you cling to your purity, young man. How afraid you are
> of dirtying your hands. Well, stay pure! Of what use will that
> be and why do you come to us? Purity is the notion of monks
> and fakirs. You intellectuals, bourgeois anarchists, make a pretext
> of it in order to do nothing. Do nothing, remain immobile, draw
> your elbows to your body, wear gloves. I have dirty hands.[17]

But Hugo is basically honest; there is nothing of the practical
politician about him. He believes in truth. One reason he joined
the communist party was that he felt his own class was one
which dealt in lies and double dealing. When he finds that
Hoederer deals with people in the same way he is disgusted
and prepares to carry out his assignment to kill the leader,
but Hoederer almost succeeds in convincing him that lies are
necessary to a political party striving for power as well as to
one which is in power. The only time when there will be no
more lies, he explains, is when there is a classless society.

Hugo, however, firmly believes that Olga, Louis, and the
other members of his faction of the party do not deal in lies,
and realizes that the only way to be one of them and therefore
of the party is by proving his capabilities and killing Hoederer.

But Hoederer's arguments sway Hugo, and when Hugo is about to tell Hoederer he will join him, the young man finds Hoederer kissing Jessica and shoots him.

Hugo has been alienated socially, intellectually, and idealistically up to this point in the play and one might expect, as he, himself, undoubtedly does, that he will at last belong because of his crime. The party, however, has received new orders from Moscow and their line has changed. They will do exactly as Hoederer had planned before he was killed by Hugo. Later, when Hugo, recently released from prison, tries to reenter the party he is told by Olga that he will be salvageable only if he forgets about his killing Hoederer or admits he killed him for some negligible reason such as jealousy. Hugo refuses because he feels Hoederer's death will be meaningless if he does so. Because he loved Hoederer, he will not permit him to become a nameless corpse killed in a fight over a woman. Hugo walks to his death as the play ends, satisfied that his own death will give meaning to that of Hoederer, and also, undoubtedly, pleased that he is dying for his principles.

Hugo differs from Oreste in one important respect. As Hoederer tells him, he does not love men; he loves principles. Whereas Oreste loves men and is willing to sacrifice himself for them to relieve their suffering, Hugo is, at least until the very end of the play, willing only to sacrifice himself to abstractions. Oreste wins, not only delivering the Argives from their guilt, but also finding himself by so doing. Hugo loses his life and in so doing finds his death justifiable because he has found meaning in life. Like *Les Mouches*, *Les Mains sales* ends on a note of hope rather than on one of despair: through Hugo's self-revelation and consequent death the ways of man have been justified. Hugo is not so positive a character as Oreste but he is decidedly more human. Oreste seems more the embodiment of an idea, the idea of *his* liberty, whereas Hugo is a man in every sense of the word, a man struggling with his own destiny.

Jessica, Olga, and Hoederer are others in the play who are extremely credible and, compared to other characters in Sartre's theatre, also rather admirable. Jessica is a brilliantly drawn person whose development from puppy love for Hugo and adolescent sophistication to mature love for Hoederer and an acute awareness of the situation about her is admirably portrayed. Olga, although a type figure, has enough human warmth about her to make her appealing. Hoederer is perhaps the finest character in the play. His interest in his work, his affectionate tolerance of Hugo, and his practical sense of values make him the most likable person in Sartre's theatre. The level to which he rises after Hugo shoots him by protecting the young man from Slick is a level that few figures in the contemporary theatre attain with such utter credibility. And yet, fine as Hoederer is, Hugo is still the central figure of *Les Mains sales* and the tragic emphasis is concentrated on him. He is as close to a tragic figure as Sartre comes in his theatre.

The anguish in which Hugo finds himself after Hoederer's death is much the same as the anguish Henri suffers after the death of François or, for that matter, as the state in which Oreste finds himself after the murder of Egisthe and Clytemnestre. There are differences among the three, however. Each has become alienated from the social group because of his crime: he has committed *his* act and this act separates him from other people. Oreste, before the murders, tells Electre that he feels too light, that there is nothing to attach him to anything concrete: he is *non-engagé*:

. . . I am too light. I must weight myself down with a heavy crime, so that I may sink straight into the abysses of Argos. . . . Let me say good-bye to that spotless lightness that was mine. Let me say good-bye to my youth.[18]

After the murders he feels the burden of his crime but he rejoices in the burden because it is his liberty. Hugo, after murdering Hoederer, is in a state of terrible doubt. His crime is not heavy to bear; it is too light. Like Oreste's it has become his destiny and it will govern his life and yet it really is not his: he has not committed himself:

. . . I wanted to attach a crime around my neck, like a rock. And I was afraid that it would be hard to bear. What an error. It is light, horribly light. It doesn't weigh. . . . It has become my destiny, you see, it governs my life from without, but I cannot see it or touch it. It isn't mine. It is a mortal malady which kills without making one suffer. . . . It's not my crime which kills me, but rather his death.[19]

It will not become *his* until after his own imminent death. Then the murder will mean something; it will justify Hoederer and it will justify himself. Henri committed his murder through pride, and he feels its weight. He says he will have to drag it with him throughout his life. Considering the circumstances, all three men committed justifiable acts. One is proud of his act and lives with it happily, the other two are ashamed of their reasons for committing their acts rather than of the acts themselves, and only their deaths can give meaning to these acts.

Sartre tells us that his next play, *Le Diable et le bon Dieu*, can pass as a complement or a sequel to *Les Mains sales*, even though it is set four hundred years earlier.[20] Goetz, the hero of *Le Diable et le bon Dieu*, is primarily an exile because of his birth. He is the bastard son of a nobleman and a peasant girl, and neither the nobility nor the peasants trust him, just as neither side would completely trust Hugo, the wealthy bourgeois who deserted his background to join the proletarian party.

The first act of *Le Diable et le bon Dieu* is a demonstration of Goetz practicing evil. Because of his bastard birth and consequent feeling of alienation from men, Goetz feels that God is the only worthy enemy. Unlike Oreste, he feels himself useless to man and therefore practices evil for evil's sake. He has men tortured and murdered, women raped by stable boys; he burns cities. Evil makes him feel light; it does not bother him. He is still *non-engagé*. Yet he has a conscience, an inverted one, to be sure, and good affects him the way evil affects others. He vaunts his practicing of evil and claims it is his alone; it is his distinguishing characteristic, just as the murder of his half-brother is his alone:

Curate, I have molded myself. Bastard I was by birth, but the fine title of fratricide I owe only to my own merits. It is mine at present, mine alone.[21]

Here we have come the whole way in Sartre's range of possibilities of human action. Oreste commits his act, which emphasizes his alienation, and is proud of it because the act is a good one. Henri's act is one committed through pride, therefore a bad one to him, and he is ashamed of it. Hugo's act was a good one, but it was committed for the wrong reasons and only his death will justify it. Goetz' murder of his brother is a bad act, and it emphasizes his exile, but he is proud of it. His act is the opposite of Oreste's. Yet both acts were committed as a visible sign of opposition to God (or Jupiter). The difference lies in the fact that, although both acts are designed to demonstrate man's essential liberty, Oreste's act is constructive and Goetz' is unjustifiably destructive. The following statement of Goetz could easily be that of an inverse Oreste:

Hatred and weakness, violence, death, chagrin, these come from man alone; this is my only empire and I am alone within it. What happens there is attributable only to me. . . . In my image God looks at himself with horror. There are twenty thousand nobles . . . but cite me another Goetz. Sometimes I imagine Hell as a desert waiting only for me.[22]

When Heinrich informs Goetz that all men perform evil acts, Goetz replies that his evil is not theirs. They perform evil as a luxury or for their own interest; he does it for the sake of doing evil. Heinrich reiterates that all men do evil and tells Goetz that doing evil is not enough to set him apart from other men:

Goetz:      Then everyone does evil?
Heinrich:  Everyone.
Goetz:      And no one has ever done good?
Heinrich:  No one.
Goetz:      Perfect. I bet you I can do it.[23]

Goetz therefore decides to do good; his decision indicates that his practicing evil was not so much opposition to God as a way of distinguishing himself in the eyes of God. Because man will not accept him, God must. His desire to do good, however, is also motivated by the same sense of inferiority. He will do what no one else can do to prove himself better than others.

Although Goetz begins his good works with the idea that evil was *he* and good is everything, he soon realizes that he is as alone doing good as he was doing evil. He finds that people detest him no matter what he does. When he finally wins the confidence of the peasants for whom he is trying to build the city of the sun, he finds he is even more alone than he was before. A peasant named Karl, who hates Goetz, wins the peasants away from him, and Goetz asks God's help because he has lost his faith in man. When the few peasants remaining with him are massacred, Goetz washes his hands of their blood and claims that man was made to be destroyed.

He will therefore destroy the man in himself and in his own flesh chastise the faults of mankind. When Heinrich finally arrives to see if Goetz has done good he is astounded to find the former conqueror half dead. Heinrich shows him that his attempts at goodness have actually been more destructive than his vices. Twenty-five thousand men have been killed because of the peasant insurrection. Goetz then concludes that there is no God:

Silence is God. Absence is God. God is the solitude of men. There was only I; I decided evil alone, alone I invented good. . . . If God exists, man is nothing; if man exists . . . Heinrich, I am going to make you see an extensive prank: God does not exist. . . . I deliver us. No more Heaven, no more Hell, nothing but the Earth.[24]

Goetz realizes that all we have on earth is our life, and he will continue his life the way he began it, as a paid soldier. Action will help him to think less. The circle has closed, and Goetz returns to evil.

He is still alienated, however, and Hilda tells him that he will always be a spiritual exile from the people of his time: "You will never be like them. Neither better, nor worse, just different."[25] If Goetz gives his lands to the peasants, a general war begins because of this gift and men are killed. The nobles mistrust his act and the peasants themselves are unsure of its import. If he destroys human lives, the only people who profit are the nobles. By desiring the absolute, either good or evil, Goetz arrives at the destruction of human lives and widens the gulf which exists between himself and his contemporaries.

Goetz is not the only spiritual exile in the play, however. Heinrich, just as Goetz, is unlike others. He is a son of the Church and a son of the poor—a bastard. Heinrich delivers the city of Worms to Goetz and leaves him the decision of destroying the city. Goetz, seeing Heinrich as another version of himself, calls him a traitor. Heinrich feels great remorse at having given the keys of the city to Goetz; but Goetz cannot restore Heinrich's purity even though he may give freedom to Worms.

When Heinrich comes to collect his wager from Goetz he finds no pleasure in killing him because Goetz is a broken man. He is shocked, however, to hear Goetz reiterate that there is no God and, afraid of the justice of man, he tries to strangle

Goetz, who kills him. Heinrich, who is similar in this respect to Henri of *Morts sans sépultures*, is afraid of men. He would rather be judged by an infinite being than by his equals who understand him only too well.

*Le Diable et le bon Dieu* is the richest-textured play of Sartre; but, unfortunately, its construction is too loose and its focus too uncertain to be a great play. The themes in it are continuations and amplifications of those we have found in the earlier plays. We find here that nothing ever changes anything,[26] that one plays himself through eternity,[27] and that all we have or can be sure of is our own life. Violence is again discussed in *Le Diable et le bon Dieu*, and we find one of the characters saying what has been hinted at in all the earlier plays, that violence is good only for those who have nothing to lose (and the Sartrian hero seldom has anything to lose).

Of the four typically Sartrian exiles—Oreste, Henri, Hugo, and Goetz—two *are* intellectuals, Oreste and Hugo; one might be called an intellectual, Henri; and one, Goetz, has great power. Goetz, Hugo, and Oreste are alienated because their birth or upbringing makes them different from the people with whom they come in contact. Each of these must perform acts in a hostile atmosphere. Each feels he has a mission. Each has a sense of social responsibility which ultimately outweighs every other consideration. Each triumphs over life and accomplishes something even when the triumph means death.

Each of the Sartrian heroes knows that he is an exile; several speak of their solitude in just those terms. Sartre has made them all superior men who arrive in a certain spot at a crucial time for an important purpose. Their exile, however, does not deter them from their purpose; instead it actually propels them into action.

And action is perhaps the chief characteristic of the Sartrian hero. It is through action alone that the hero can justify his existence and prove his own worth. All of the heroes battle tyranny, whether it be earthly or celestial, to improve man's condition. Oreste comes to the aid of the guilt-ridden Argives; Henri saves the lives of sixty Maquisards. Hugo would like to help his fellow man improve his condition and joins the communist party for that very reason, but he will not compromise with his principles and dies not disillusioned but perplexed. He has a more difficult time than Oreste, who is really only a concrete image of abstract ideas, because he does not have Oreste's placid self-assurance. He questions before he acts, as Oreste does not. Goetz tries to help man ameliorate his condition but he finds that neither of the extremes, good or evil, is practical, and he actually kills more men through his actions than he would have had he not acted at all.

Although, like most heroes in the modern drama, Sartre's heroes feel great personal solitude, even when they are with other people, they do not disintegrate as readily as the characters of Lenormand or Anouilh. They remain essentially healthy human beings through the plays, and if any change has been effected at all during the play it is usually for the better. Of the four Sartrian heroes one is an outstanding figure in the modern theatre—Hugo, who is a credible and admirable person. He is a man, not a puppet being manipulated by Sartre as are Goetz and Oreste, who are too much the embodiments of ideas to be entirely believable.

It is unfortunate that Sartre's heroes too often seem to be abstractions created by the author purposely to illustrate men who strive to integrate humanity by committing themselves through an action which is also an abstraction. These characters ultimately fail to become great tragic heroes because of this very abstractness. They are likable puppets, but the human element is too often missing in their characters.

Whether the alienation of the heroes of Sartre is as painful as that of other characters in the modern French drama is debatable. These heroes can forget their personal solitude in action, as few other exiles in the contemporary theatre can. But insofar as they are superior men their alienation is more painful to us than that of others because we not only sympathize with their anguish but admire intellectually what they represent.

The only other play of major significance related to the existentialist theatre is Camus' *Caligula* in which there is a critique by implication of existentialism, and also a strange alienated hero.

Although its first stage presentation was in 1945, Camus' *Caligula* was written in 1938. Between these two dates Camus had published *Le Mythe de Sisyphe*, a long philosophical essay in which he defines his position with regard to the existentialists and states his own theory of the absurd. Aside from being an important philosophical tract, *Le Mythe de Sisyphe* is also a key to the first two plays of Camus, *Caligula* and *Le Malentendu*. It explains to a large extent the philosophical implications of these plays, and implies the author's attitude towards his characters, thus enriching their meaning, if not their value, as works of art. It also casts light on the existentialist problems expressed in *Caligula*.

*Caligula* poses a major problem because the hero, the title character, is portrayed with such profundity and yet with such an illusory quality that on first acquaintance he is completely baffling. Is he the Absurd Man Camus speaks of in *Le Mythe de Sisyphe* who has gone wrong? Or is he merely a madman whose destiny has ensnared him? Or is he more than that? And if so, what?

Upon his first appearance Caligula appears to be a man whose mind has been affected by some personal calamity, and we have been previously informed by several secondary characters that his mistress, Drusilla, has died and that he is prey to the profoundest grief because of her death. When we first see him, however, he is beyond the stage of grief. He says:

This world as it is is not bearable. So I need the moon or happiness or immortality, something which is mad perhaps, but which is not of this world.[28]

This is the first of many indications of Caligula's madness. But immediately the problem arises: is it madness? There is a terrible lucidity in all that he says or does, as Cheréa points out, an almost superhuman lucidity and logic that defy opposition. Having experienced the death of Drusilla, he believes he has found truth and explains that her death is only the sign of a truth that makes it necessary for him to have the moon. The truth he has discovered is that men die, and that they are not happy because of the capriciousness of the irrational world and its complete unintelligibility to man. Therefore, as defiance of the irrational and/or whatever gods may be, he decides to make use of his new-found liberty (which he claims derives from his discovery that the world is unimportant) in order to disown both man and the world. And the play on one level is a demonstration of Caligula's capricious yet logical madness in denying both the value of human life and the world.

On another and more philosophical level, however, Caligula becomes more understandable. He begins as an ordinary man, albeit an emperor, who suddenly comes into contact with the blind irrationality of the universe. Camus calls this confrontation of the wild longing for clarity, which is in the human heart, with the irrational world the birth of the absurd, and:

From the moment absurdity is recognized, it becomes a passion, the most harrowing of all. But whether or not one can live with one's passions, whether or not one can accept their law, which is to burn the heart they simultaneously exalt—that is the whole question.[29]

The realization of the absurd terrifies Caligula, and rather than accept his freedom within the confines of human life he attempts the impossible of which getting the moon is the symbol. (It is also a symbol on another plane of Caligula's madness.) The impossible consists in rendering human life as meaningless as blind fate does. In attempting to do this, and thus pronouncing his alienation from mankind (and this is crucial), Caligula becomes an aspect of the irrational world itself, and therefore not completely human. His actions thus become those of a monster. He has adopted an axiom which might be stated thus: what you can't conquer or understand you become or join. Caligula, paradoxically, understands completely the irrationality of the universe and man's relation to it, but by accepting the world's irrationality and not revolting against it, as the Absurd Man should, he becomes a failure to his creator, for Camus claims that the absurd has meaning only insofar as it is not agreed to. Caligula will defy the absurd only insofar as he becomes it.

And yet his becoming a monster is efficacious in one way. His subjects when they come into contact with him, like the Absurd Man when he comes into contact with the irrational world, are made to think. Cheréa says: "Let's grant at least that this man exercises an undeniable influence. He makes one think. Insecurity is what makes one think. And that is why so many hatreds follow it."[30]

Camus speaks in *Le Mythe de Sisyphe* of the failure of the existentialist philosophers to be consistently logical, and he attacks them again in the person of Caligula, for in this respect at least *Caligula* is a criticism of them. In the work of the existentialist philosophers one finds, Camus claims, that the theme of the irrational is reason becoming confused and escaping by negating itself, whereas the absurd is lucid reasoning noting its limits. As with the existentialists, Caligula's reason negates itself (as he himself realizes at the end of the play). He says: "I didn't take the right road. I ended up nowhere. My liberty is not the right one."[31] And he dies by the swords of the conspirators without having found his real liberty.

Caligula has no courage, for courage is what teaches a man to live without appeal and to get along with what he has; his reason informs him of his limits. Caligula, however, does not accept his limits, and therefore his reasoning is poor. He believes that all actions are equivalent, but he does not always recognize the value of those actions.

One might conclude at this point that *Caligula* is a paradoxical play in which a man who has reached the point of encountering the absurd, the understanding and acceptance of which would make him the Absurd Man par excellence, becomes instead the irrational world itself. This is especially evident when Caligula is contrasted with Cheréa, the *raisonneur* of the play, for Cheréa illustrates the Absurd Man who thinks clearly and who has ceased to hope.

Caligula, although the hero of the play, is not a tragic figure, nor is the play a tragedy, nor did Camus intend it to be so, if one may judge from his remarks on tragedy in *Le Mythe de Sisyphe*. Camus claims, and this is not unlike the classical theory of tragedy, that the tragic figure is a man who comes in contact with fate and triumphs over it, even though the triumph be in death. But to Camus, the hero to be tragic must be conscious of his fate. Caligula, although he believes himself conscious of the problems of the universe, is deluded by his colossal egoism, and his unlimited power accentuates and continues the delusion. He is tragic only insofar as a monster can be tragic. He is not conscious of his fate, and he does not care about it. His sole ambition is to equal the gods or the irrational world in power. And in the moments in the play when he is human, and there are several, he is only pathetic because he understands so little of man's condition and places so little value on human life and the act of living.

Camus, speaking of living, in *Le Mythe de Sisyphe* says:

Living is keeping the absurd alive. Keeping it alive is, above all, contemplating it. Unlike Eurydice, the absurd dies only when we turn away from it. One of the only coherent philosophical positions is thus revolt. It is a constant confrontation between man and his own obscurity. It is an insistence upon an impossible transparency. It challenges the world anew every second. Just as danger provided man the unique opportunity of seizing awareness. so metaphysical revolt extends awareness to the whole of experience. It is that constant presence of man in his own eyes. It is not aspiration, for it is devoid of hope. The revolt is the certainty of a crushing fate, without the resignation that ought to accompany it.[32]

This sums up Caligula as a character. He is not an absurd man because he resigns himself to and becomes his fate—and he is not tragic in the Aristotelian sense either—because the tragic figure must battle his fate actively and in the fray, though conquered, give dignity to man or meaning to life. Camus' theories of tragedy are closer to those of the ancient Greeks than are those of any of his contemporaries. Yet in *Caligula*, and it seems consciously so, he has not created a tragedy but has rather written an indictment of the excesses to which a basically ordinary yet intelligent man can turn by alienating himself from his world and ignoring the value of human life and man's essential dignity.

# Conclusion

ALIENATION has been a dominant theme in the works of France's most notable playwrights since the First World War. That it is also an important theme in the works of many minor playwrights may be seen by reading such plays as *La Souriante Madame Beudet* of Amiel and Obey, *Le Paquebot Tenacity* and *Le Pèlerin* of Vildrac, *Martine* and *L'Invitation au voyage* of Jean-Jacques Bernard, *Le Cocu magnifique* of Crommelynck, *Oedipe* of Gide, and the various plays of Cocteau and Salacrou. This list could be continued, and when completed it would indicate that the alienated hero is a major figure in French drama since 1920.

The exiles in the contemporary French theatre cannot be considered noble people in the sense that an Oedipus, an Othello, or a Polyeucte is noble. The closest to the classic ideal of the noble hero are Sartre's Oreste, Giraudoux's Electre, and Anouilh's Antigone, and even they in comparison with the great characters of the past seem rather contrived and ineffectual. Few of the modern heroes and heroines are admirable people. Most of them are hyper-sensitive, and although hyper-sensitivity is usually an adjunct of the tragic hero, it is, in the modern drama, combined with egocentricity and eccentricity to such an extent that it almost ceases to become a virtue.

The dramatis personae of the contemporary French drama have been alienated from society for various reasons. The aristocrat has lost his place in the social hierarchy because of the social revolutions of the past century and a half. Because he will not accept the world as it is he is cast aside to deteriorate in solitude. The homosexuals and the mentally ill heroes of Lenormand are alienated because society does not tolerate aberration. The heroines of Giraudoux and the characters of Anouilh refuse a corrupt world. The Sartrian heroes, because of their intelligence, are alienated from a society which is overrun by superstition and social injustice.

Each of these exiles is a reflection on the society which has cast him out. The fact that the society to which they belong has seen fit not to tolerate their aberrations, combined with the fact that so many of these characters deny their world, is a comment upon our age. Has any period of world drama ever damned its own epoch as much as ours? The sickness of the world is shown only too clearly by its rejection of the aristocrats, the homosexuals, and many of the heroes of Sartre, people who might have contributed greatly had they not been rejected. Those who were not cast aside by their world but who turned their backs on it provide just as damning a commentary. As much as we may dislike the heroes of Montherlant and Lenormand, their protests, like those of the characters of Anouilh and Giraudoux, against contemporary existence ring true in many instances. The hypocrisy, greed, and corruption which they find are disquieting. Existence appears to be more trouble than it is worth.

Established order usually seems to win the battle with its exiles, and the victory helps to give the modern theatre its distinctly pessimistic overtones. Society wins because most of its exiles are passive figures who disintegrate in solitude. Those characters who do act, such as the heroes and heroines of Sartre, Camus, Anouilh, and Giraudoux, are usually forced to choose death because they seldom can attain their objectives in their society, and their deaths only prove once again that in the drama, at least, existence is intolerable to a person of superior sensibility. The same social conditions as before remain after their deaths, and the universe has not been justified. Most of these heroes protest strongly against their society; most of them realize that their inability or unwillingness to adjust to it is the direct cause of their alienation. They may be right in placing the blame on society, but much of the blame lies in their own weaknesses, too. Had they been less egocentric and eccentric they might have been more admirable. The heroes of Lenormand, Montherlant, Curel, Bourdet, and Martin du Gard would rather complain about their various maladies and the injustices of society than accept themselves for what they are and then try to liberalize the codes of that society.

Thus, one of the distinguishing traits of the contemporary

theatre seems to become apparent. Its heroes and heroines in general appear to be failures. With the exception of the heroes of Sartre and Giraudoux's Electre, they never seem to achieve anything. This at first glance is the obvious conclusion. What appears evident, however, upon reconsideration of the plays is that the society itself is the failure rather than the heroes and heroines. Each author treated in this study damns the contemporary world, and damns it in a way unfamiliar to the classic author. In the classical drama society, the established order, the universe, or whatever one wishes to call it, is a worthy opponent of and foil for its heroes and heroines. Existence, as well as the hero, has meaning. At the conclusion of a classical play the universe and man are justified. In the modern theatre not only are many of the heroes sick but the society which has spawned them seems even sicker. It is almost invariably painted black. What we seem to have learned at the conclusion of these plays is that the world is a social hydra which kills or forces into exile not only its non-conformists but also its superior people. We learn that it is hypocritical and afraid of its own tendencies toward the very things it persecutes. We learn that greed is rampant, that perversity and perversion are prevalent, that power and religion are corrupt. We learn, in fact, that society is sicker than its exile-heroes. It becomes the *bête noire* of the modern theatre, and inasmuch as many of its exile-heroes are forced to choose death because they feel impotent to accomplish anything in the world, there is little wonder that the dramatic authors are pessimistic. We ask ourselves when we finish reading their works if there is any hope short of complete destruction—such as we find at the end of *Electre*.

This pessimism is, of course, black romanticism, an inversion of the optimism of the nineteenth century. Many of the same social injustices which existed then still exist and in more or less the same form. But authors like Hugo, Lamartine, and Renan envisaged a bright future which would come through the power of science. Science has arrived and the aura of the times is hardly bright. Perhaps our authors are being more realistic by being pessimistic. But *we* become depressed, too, after observing their heroes and heroines. Negation of life seems to rule the day. In the drama death seems to be the only alternative for the sensitive person. Life is something to be merely tolerated. It cannot be enjoyed: there is always a stray dog suffering on some stage, and that dog is society.

If our authors damn their world and see it as unjustifiable, as many of them do, then life has no meaning. The sacrifices that the dramatis personae of our modern drama make are therefore meaningless and their deaths are not tragic. Tragedy in modern drama would seem to be that of a condemned universe for which there is no hope, rather than the tragedy of a particular man or woman as it is in the classical drama.

Like the heroes of Greek and Shakespearean drama, the modern exile-hero feels his loneliness. His isolation is a burden which is often too heavy to be borne. But the modern hero also tends to be an egotist whose personal problems assume an importance which does not always seem to be justifiable. The heroes of Montherlant, Lenormand, Sartre, Bourdet, Martin du Gard, Curel, Camus, and even some of the heroines of Anouilh and Giraudoux feel that they are, if not at the center, certainly near the center of the universe. Their unawareness, in many instances, of the problems of the world tends to make them either case histories or abstractions. The few characters who do not fit into either of these categories, such as Eurydice, Antigone, Thérèse, or Isabelle, do not seem to have the stature of great tragic heroes. Even when these heroes and heroines are aware of the problems of their world, their world is so corrupt that they can do nothing for it except, as in the case of Electre, destroy it.

Few of the characters in contemporary French drama seem able to communicate with their fellows. They are misunderstood and they misunderstand. Their plaints reverberate through each play until the sound becomes as monotonous and expected as the sound of subway trains pulling into a station. Their isolation is overwhelming to them and important to use because it denotes that as social beings they are impotent.

Because of their personal isolation and the cruelty of their world to them, as well as because of their egocentricity, many of our modern heroes and heroines are, or tend to be, sadistic. Some are consciously so. Such are Rougé, Laurency, Sarterre, Fearon, Inès, Goetz, Irène, Alvaro, and Ferrante. Others are unconsciously sadistic, unaware of the pain they are causing others. Among these are Frantz, Judith, Hélène, and Lucie.

They seem so absorbed by themselves and their own problems that they hurt others with an almost terrifying regularity.

The major emotions do not often appear in any of the heroes and heroines of the modern drama. Few of them are capable of experiencing love, not only the love of a Juliet or an Othello, but even the guilty love of a Phèdre. Love does not exist for the heroes of Sartre, Lenormand, or Montherlant. Many of Giraudoux's heroines seem incapable of experiencing this emotion. The homosexuals seldom seem capable of achieving love with either sex; the aristocrats are too much interested in other problems to be at all concerned with love. Only in Anouilh's plays do we find any of the characters experiencing love, and in his drama it is distinctly adolescent.

Hatred, jealousy, avarice, even pride are seldom found in these heroes and heroines. No one vice or virtue towers over most of these plays. Neuroses and psychoses are found nearly everywhere and, of course, these, or the awareness of them, seem characteristic of the twentieth century, even though we do find them in Euripides and Racine. But the expressions of these individual neuroses alone do not make great tragedy. There are other, more admirable qualities in the characters of Racine and Euripides which are seldom found in the modern drama. At best, the protrayal of these neuroses and psychoses has given us fascinating case histories but seldom, if ever, tragedy.

The means of escape for the various exile-heroes of our drama differ from author to author, and even from play to play. The aristocrat can live in the reflected glory of a past which everyone but him has forgotten. He can retire to an ivory tower and ponder the greatness of his ancestors when the world becomes too much with him. Or, like the heroes of Montherlant, he can ignore the world and contemplate the Deity or his own magnificence. Or, he can hope to find and yet fail to find in sexual promiscuity forgetfulness of an overwhelming reality—the society in which he lives.

Death seems to be the major escape for the homosexual. Thierry, Ian in Julien Green's *Sud*, Martha in *The Children's Hour* commit suicide. The heroes of Lenormand find escape in flights from reality. Some become interested in the supernatural. Others flee to exotic countries. Some commit suicide; still others indulge in vices such as stealing, dope, murder, and sexual aberrations. None of them can live happily in society.

The means of escape for the heroines of Giraudoux is in ignoring what seems unimportant and in following an abstract concept such as integral justice, purity, and the like. Some like Lia and Isabelle ignore the world and seek death. Death is the only escape for the heroes and heroines of Anouilh because only in death can they find the perfection they seek. Sartre's heroes find escape in action, and they alone in the modern drama seem to do anything concrete. They, like Electre, fight against the evils in their society and try to ameliorate that society. They alone, with several heroines of Giraudoux, come close to making us aware of the occasional greatness of man. And yet, they fail to become great tragic heroes because they appear to be merely abstractions in Sartre's mind.

The result of the exile of these various characters is incomprehensible waste. Death without meaning and disintegration in solitude seem to be the only results of the exile of our heroes. The human wrecks, dead and alive, who appear on the stage at the final curtain are not merely depressing; they are horrible and terrifying. We pity them but emerge from the theatre feeling only the digust with our world that our authors feel. We have not, as we have in the classic drama, learned much about the nobility of human nature. We have seen little of man's majesty. We have observed some pathetic people protesting against a cruel world, and usually being defeated by it. And their defeat seems only to prove that their creators appear to believe that the finer things in life cannot and probably never will be attained.

If, as I have mentioned before, the authors of our drama are portraying their own alienation from the corrupt world, which they attack in the persons of their heroes, then the modern drama might be said to be an outgrowth of the romantic drama and possibly its culmination. Critic after critic tells us that Lenormand's characters are based on his own life and personality, that Anouilh's heroes experience his emotions and react in life as he did. Montherlant, himself, tells us that his characters are he. These men, and the others discussed, are undoubtedly sensitive men, and the fact that they feel their alienation from society is obvious in their writings. To express this alienation these authors seem to have created characters who are more sensitive than others to the problems of life, but perhaps because the authors have been too close to their creations and not objective enough about the world in which they live, they have failed to create true tragedy.

In many respects the modern dramatic literature of France might be called adolescent. So many playwrights portray the feeling of exile and of conflict with the world and the social group not only as an attribute of their characters but of themselves as well that they give us good reason to term this drama adolescent. What critics have called the mature acceptance of the world or at least the feeling that the universe has its own justification, as has man, is seldom seen in the modern drama. The egocentric attitude of the various characters in many modern plays is another trait of adolescence found in the plays of our day which is lacking in the classical drama. Even though their pride might tend to make them appear completely egocentric, Oedipus and Macbeth are aware of the world. There are universal laws which are over and above themselves; they are not the most important facets of existence as so many modern characters seem to feel themselves to be. The modern hero, like the adolescent, tries to remold society rather than himself. He is uncompromising. The classic dramatists seemed to see that society could not be remolded, but that man could occasionally prove his own dignity.

In the modern drama society becomes a *bête noire* while modern dramatists bewail the fact that it cannot be changed. The very desperation of some of their heroes and heroines makes this all too obvious. When our modern heroes do try to remold society, they resort to violence, like the heroes of Sartre, Giraudoux, and some of the heroes and heroines of Lenormand and Anouilh. Murder and wholesale destruction seem to be the only way of cleansing a dirtied world. Of all the modern dramatists Giraudoux, perhaps, is the only one who realizes the folly of this. The various interpretations evoked by the conscious irony of the conclusion of Electre, "Cela s'appelle l'aurore," would seem to indicate this. He smiles ironically but most of the other dramatists resort to the blackest pessimism because the world is, and probably always will be, imperfect.

This dissatisfaction with the world is another trait of the adolescent who wants to make the world into his image. The classical dramatists such as Sophocles might smile ruefully and say that it is a pity that man will never be perfect, but we must make the best of what we have, since experience has shown us that man will probably never change. And then Sophocles and the other Greek dramatists, as well as Shakespeare, will prove that man can have dignity and that life can occasionally have meaning. The pessimism is still there but in their works some value in human life and in the universe is shown. And one leaves the theatre after witnessing their plays feeling, if not elated, certainly purged of baser emotions. On the other hand, one leaves the modern theatre despondent and pessimistic. The characters portrayed there have had to escape from their problems by suicide, actual transplanting of themselves to another country, or delving into devious perversions. Realizing that they cannot attain their absolutes, they prefer death, but choosing death because life is corrupt would seem to be negative and a way of avoiding eternal human problems. Thus, in many respects this literature seems to be adolescent. The seemingly most mature of its authors, Giraudoux, comes closer to the outlook of the classical dramatists than any of his contemporaries, and yet even he has failed to give us a tragic hero comparable to the creations of Sophocles and Shakespeare.

# Notes

## CHAPTER I

1. Joseph Wood Krutch, *The Modern Temper*, 141.
2. *Ibid.*, 119 f.
3. *Ibid.*, 125.
4. *Ibid.*, 128.
5. *Ibid.*, 132.

## CHAPTER II

1. Curel, *Théâtre complet*, II, 161.
2. *Ibid.*, 161 f.
3. *Ibid.*, 226 f.
4. *Ibid.*, 240.
5. *Ibid.*, 252 f.
6. *See* Jones, Robert E., "The Early Heroines of Tennessee Williams," *Modern Drama*, December, 1959.
7. The Abbé himself claims that his love is pure. One wonders, however, if his homosexual tendencies—and his attraction to the young boy is a homosexual one—are not more those of the poet of *Les Nourritures terrestres* than those of man's love for his fellow man. In any case, pure to him seems to signify the absence of overt experiences, and this idea is hardly a criterion for the purity of a love.
8. Simon, *Procès du héros*, 97 f.
9. Cf. Jacques de La Prade, *Le Théâtre de Montherlant*, 11.
10. Montherlant, *Théâtre complet*, II, 22.
11. Cf. LaPrade, *op. cit.*, 19.
12. Montherlant, *Théâtre complet*, II, 41.
13. Cf. Simon, *Témoins de l'homme*, 108.
14. Cf. LaPrade, *op. cit.*, 32.
15. Montherlant, *Théâtre complet*, II, 126.
16. *Ibid.*, II, 132.
17. *Ibid.*, II, 61.
18. *Ibid.*, IV, 20.
19. *Ibid.*, IV, 77.
20. *Ibid.*, IV, 37.
21. *Ibid.*, IV, 38.
22. *Ibid.*, IV, 39.
23. *Ibid.*, IV, 49.
24. *Ibid.*, IV, 54.
25. *Ibid.*, IV, 58.
26. *Ibid.*, IV, cf. 67.
27. *Ibid.*, I, 82.
28. *Ibid.*, I, 61 f.
29. *Ibid.*, I, 63.
30. *Ibid.*, I, 102.
31. *Ibid.*, I, 81.
32. LaPrade, *op. cit.*, 131.
33. Montherlant, *Théâtre complet*, I, 128.
34. Bendz, "Le Désespoir dans l'oeuvre récente de Montherlant," in *Montherlant, Bourreau de soi-même*, 148.
35. Jaccard, *Trois Contemporains*, 79.
36. Montherlant, *Service inutile*, 20.
37. Montherlant, *Textes sous une occupation*, 162 f.

## CHAPTER III

1. *La Dame aux camélias* of Alexandre Dumas fils depicted a courtesan sympathetically. The protest aroused by this play can best be seen in Émile Augier's *Le Mariage d'Olympe*, written as an answer to Dumas fils. Augier's play shows the disas-

trous results of treating a courtesan kindly.

2. Mario Praz in *The Romantic Agony* speculates about the homosexual bases of many of the Byronic heroes and their literary progeny, but inasmuch as the audience of the day seemed unaware of them, or ignored them, they do not concern us here.

3. The most famous scene of homosexual love in the Greek theatre, and the best loved by the Athenians, was the love scene between Orestes and Pylades in Euripides' *Iphigenia in Tauris*. H. M. Grube, in his *Drama of Euripides* (p. 21), asks, "Do we not realize · that emotionally Pylades and Orestes are lovers . . . and that the scenes between them in *Iphigenia in Tauris* and *Orestes* are love scenes?"

4. Norwood, *Greek Tragedy*, 174.

5. The homosexual basis of this play, *The Lovers of Achilles*, is also suggested not only by the title but by the contents of the few fragments which have come down to us. See Sophocles, *Plays and Fragments*, ed. by Lewis Campbell.

6. Havelock Ellis, *Studies in the Psychology of Sex*, I, part 4, 36.

7. *Ibid.*, 32.

8. The homosexual aspects of the characters of Marlowe's Edward II, Shakespeare's Richard II, Racine's Hippolyte, and the fops of the Elizabethan and Restoration plays have been noticed by many critics. But homosexuality as such is not a major element in any of these plays, even though it may be an aspect of the character of the protagonist.

9. Jean Jacques Rousseau, *Oeuvres complètes*, XIV, 100 ff.

10. Voltaire, *Dictionnaire philosophique*, Article, "Amour nommé socratique."

11. Paul Morand has recently discussed homosexuality as the dominating characteristic of Octave in Stendhal's *Armance*. (N. N. R. F., Paris, Mai, 1953.)

12. Henry James in *The Pupil* and Thomas Mann in *Death in Venice* also wrote of homosexuality.

13. Much of this literature is mentioned or discussed in Daniel Webster Cory's *The Homosexual in America*.

14. Aldridge, *After the Lost Generation*, 101.

15. See Henri Peyre, *The Contemporary French Novel*, 32 ff.

16. It was during the same period that England and the United States witnessed their first contemporary plays dealing with the sexual deviant. In the early thirties *The Green Bay Tree* was produced. This play by Mordaunt Shairp is concerned with an elderly man and the young boy whom he adopts. The youth spurns the love of a fine girl and becomes exactly like his protector, an effeminate and sybaritic aesthete. Lillian Hellman's *The Children's Hour*, produced in New York in 1934, provoked a scandal at its first performance but was allowed to complete its run. In this melodrama a vicious young girl unjustly accuses her two school mistresses of Lesbianism. Tragedy inevitably results when one of the women commits suicide and the other loses her life's goal. In many of the plays of Tennessee Williams, and especially in *A Streetcar Named Desire* and *Camino Real*, homosexuality is a subsidiary theme. Even more recently the Goetz adaptation for the stage of *The Immoralist* and Robert Anderson's *Tea and Sympathy* have been produced on Broadway, and both have dealt with homosexuality.

17. Mme d'Aiguines never appears on stage. Bourdet's subtle technique here eliminates what might become an embarrasing

situation if the two women were to confront each other.

18. Bourdet, *La Prisonnière*, 48. Jacques' role as Irène's savior is indicated by her time and again in the play. "You must not abandon me! . . . I am so lonely, so miserable! . . . I have only you, Jacques! Only you can help me." (48) "If you don't help me now, immediately . . . it will be too late." (115).

19. *Ibid.*, 170.

20. *Ibid.*, 173.

21. *Ibid.*, 101.

22. *Ibid.*, 102.

23. *Ibid.*, 116 f.

24. *Ibid.*, 171.

25. Gide, *The Journals*, tr. by Justin O'Brien, vol. III, 200 f.

26. In Gide's *Journal* for November 12, 1931, there is the following entry (p. 204):
"Have oneself treated—or kill oneself. No other possible solution to the problem raised by the case of Roger Martin du Gard's *Un Taciturne*—his cousin declares peremptorily in an article (moreover almost excellent) in *Les Nouvelles litteraires*. As if all the 'Thierrys' we know, and all those we do not know, had not each one found a personal solution. As if, in the play itself, Roger Martin du Gard had not taken care to make his Armand ('the only reasonable character in the play') exclaim: 'You cannot make me believe that if Joë had reciprocated. . . .' Mme Théo remarked very judiciously that it is not only the discovery of his own love that pushes Thierry to suicide, but perhaps also, but perhaps above all, immediately recognizing it to be hopeless; and his jealousy."
This remark of Mme Théo is interesting to conjecture upon. If Joë had reciprocated would Thierry have committed suicide? This question might be of some importance because a man

of Thierry's stolid nature and inveterate habits would probably never have committed any overt act which would bespeak his love for the youth, who could pass through life as the favorite of the older man without ever knowing that Thierry was in love with him.

Suicide is the only solution to Thierry. He could never have risked his own pride by confessing his love to Joë, who would probably have repulsed him. If this had happened he would definitely have taken his own life. Because of his age Thierry is perhaps more susceptible to violent emotions than a younger person might be, and the shock of recognizing his own homosexuality causes in him an emotion so profound that in a moment of weakness he loses his equilibrium and shoots himself. When one considers his age and the life he has led his action becomes more understandable.

Perhaps most important of all is the fact that other people than he know of his tendencies. Armand certainly does, and they are suspected by Wanda, who is a Lesbian. Thierry has been a solid citizen who has upheld the moral code all his life. He would undoubtedly demand punishment for anyone else who broke it and, being a just man, realized he would be subject to punishment himself for transgressing. He could no longer live with himself, much less with others who knew of his weakness. Thierry is not flexible. He sees things as black and white and is unaware of the intervening shades. Since he has transgressed, he must die.

27. Martin du Gard, *Un Taciturne*, 28.

28. *Ibid.*, 21.

29. *Ibid.*, 26.

30. Gide in his *Journal*, on December 24, 1931, discusses Wan-

da and her physical distaste for Thierry (208 f.)

31. Joë's trick of entering Thierry's office and then getting a job resembles to a surprising degree the trick of Bernard Profitendieu in Gide's *Les Faux-Monnayeurs* (1926). Bernard gets Edouard's suitcase, reads his diary, goes to see Laura, and then boldly offers himself to be Edouard's secretary. Such a combination of dash with imagination in an attractive person would be certain to conquer a susceptible man, or even an unsusceptible one, and Thierry and Edouard are conquered.

32. Gide's *Journal* again throws some light on Martin du Gard's intentions here. Entry for Oct. 4, 1931 (III, 193-94): "Roger complains of not being able to find a young actor who is sufficiently attractive physically. X., who offers himself for the role, is intelligent and charming; but, says Roger: 'No one in the audience will ever have a desire to kiss him on the mouth'."

33. The stage directions read when Thierry speaks to Wanda, thinking her to be the object of Joë's affections (Martin du Gard, *Un Taciturne*, p. 92): "To Wanda in a rather irritated voice:"

34. The irony in this passage is remarkable. Thierry's reactions are justified psychologically because unconsciously he relates his as yet unconscious desire for Joë with his previous failures with women. The irony might be called celestial irony, because it puts the spectator in the place of a God who foresees what will happen and its implications long before Thierry sees them.

35. This passage is very suggestive of the passages in Gide's *Et nunc manet in te* in which he speaks of his love for his wife, Madeleine.

36. Martin du Gard, *Un Taciturne*, 103.
37. *Ibid.*, 107.
38. *Ibid.*, 205.
39. *Ibid.*, 209.
40. *Ibid.*, 218 f.
41. *Ibid.*, 222 f.
42. René Lalou in his *Martin du Gard* (p. 21) says that Armand has the role of *raisonneur*: "he defends the rights of health, of humanity."
43. Cf. Martin du Gard, *Un Taciturne*, 223 f.
44. René Lalou finds, justly, that Thierry "has committed the error of taking a convention for a law and making a bogy of it." (Lalou, *Martin du Gard*, 21.)
45. Martin du Gard, Un Taciturne, 128.
46. This is a theme that runs through most modern plays and will be discussed at greater length in other chapters of this book.
47. Martin du Gard, *Un Taciturne*, 130.
48. *Ibid.*, 34 f.
49. *Ibid.*, 52 f.
50. Martin du Gard, *Un Taciturne*, 53.
51. Wanda, who has strong Lesbian tendencies even if she does not express them to Isabelle, is also a sexual exile.
52. Martin du Gard, *Un Taciturne*, 190.
53. Gide, *Journals*, III, 194.
54. *Ibid.*, 199.
55. Lenormand, *Théâtre complet*, II, 90.
56. *Ibid.*, IX, 224.
57. *Ibid.*, III, 178.
58. *Ibid.*, II, 55.
59. *Ibid.*, IV, 127.
60. *Ibid.*, III, 273.
61. *Ibid.*, IV, 6.
62. *Ibid.*, II, 80.
63. *Ibid.*, III, 239.
64. *Ibid.*, II, 65.
65. *Ibid.*, II, 63.
66. *Ibid.*, II, 64.
67. *Ibid.*, II, 252.
68. *Ibid.*, VII, 178.
69. *Ibid.*, X, 55-56.

70. The defeat of these characters is tragic to Lenormand. It is not tragic to the reader who demands that for stage heroes to be tragic they battle actively against their fate. The character who is a pawn of circumstances and who does not struggle against them is scarcely even admirable.

71. This may be, as Serge Radine suggests in his book on Lenormand (p. 95), because Lenormand's characters are only forms of his own personality: "His characters are scarcely, one has not underlined it enough, anything but concrete forms of himself."

72. Cf. Lenormand, *Théâtre complet*, I, 30; II, 130; II, 254; IV, 44.

73. *Ibid.*, I, 199.

74. *Ibid.*, I, 125 f.

75. *Ibid.*, VIII, 14. Cf. also VI, 15.

76. *Ibid.*, II, 214.

77. John Palmer, *Studies in the Contemporary Theatre*, 75.

78. Cf. Lenormand, *Théâtre complet*, IV, 225.

79. *Ibid.*, IV, 230 f.

80. *Ibid.*, IV, 167.

81. *Ibid.*, IV, 134.

82. *Ibid.*, III, 188.

83. *Ibid.*, IV, 4.

84. *Ibid.*, IV, 64 f.

85. *Le Simoun*, *A L'Ombre du mal*, *Terre de Satan*.

86. *L'Homme et ses fantômes*, *Le Mangeur de rêves*.

87. *Le Temps est un songe* is set in Holland; *La Folle du ciel* in Norway.

88. *Le Lâche*, *La Dent rouge*, *L'Innocente* are set exclusively in the Alps. Scenes in *Le Mangeur de rêves*, *L'Homme et ses fantômes* and *Les Trois Chambres* are also placed there.

89. *L'Amour magicien*.

90. *La Maison des remparts*.

91. *Asie*, *Pacifique*.

92. *Une Vie secrète*, *L'Homme et ses fantômes*, *Mixture*, *Crépuscule du théâtre* and *Les Trois Chambres* are partially set there.

93. Lenormand, *Théâtre complet*, II, 37.

94. *Ibid.*, II, 39.

95. *Ibid.*, II, 147.

96. *Ibid.*, II, 165.

97. Lenormand, *Théâtre complet*, VII, 108. The passages in italics are in English in the French edition.

98. Cf. Serge Radine, 95 f.

## CHAPTER IV

1. Jacques Carot, "Délivrance d'Anouilh," 42.

2. Anouilh, *Nouvelles Pièces noires*, 125.

3. Cf. Robert O. J. Van Nuffell, "Jean Anouilh," *Rivista di letterature moderne*, 82.

4. Anouilh, *Pièces roses*, 45.

5. Anouilh, *Nouvelles Pièces noires*, 204.

6. Anouilh, *Pièces noires*, 464.

7. Cf. Van Nuffell, "Jean Anouilh," 81.

8. Monime uses this phrase in *L'Hermine*, *Pièces noires*, 79. Thérèse, in *La Sauvage* uses it several times; *Pièces noires*, 151, 167, 169, 175, 198, 204. Eurydice uses it; *Pièces noires*, 397. Orphée uses it; *Pièces noires*, 398, 417, 456. Gustave uses it in *Le Bal des voleurs*; *Pièces roses*, 49, 81. Antigone uses it; *Nouvelles Pièces noires*, 157. Medée, too, uses it; *Nouvelles Pièces noires*, 388, 395. In *Jézabel* Marc uses it; *Nouvelles Pièces noires*, 56.

9. Anouilh, *Nouvelles Pièces noires*, 84.

10. Anouilh, *Pièces noires*, 36.

11. Cf. Jean Didier, *A la Rencontre de Jean Anouilh*, 14-15.

12. Anouilh, *Pièces noires*, 170.

13. Edward O. Marsh, *Jean Anouilh*, 57.

14. Anouilh, *Pièces noires*, 198.

15. *Ibid.*, 256.

16. Anouilh, *Nouvelles Pièces noires*, 184.

17. Anouilh, *Pièces noires*, 381.

18. *Ibid.*, 433.

19. *Ibid.*, 481.

20. *Ibid.*, 481.

21. *Ibid.*, 428 f.

22. *Ibid.*, 464.
23. *Ibid.*, 499.
24. One is led to wonder whether Gaston is really different from the youth he was before the war. He certainly seems a less unhappy person, but his essential egotism, his self-centeredness, and even his sadism remain. Anouilh believes that one can never escape from the past, and Gaston cannot escape completely from his. There is a certain permanence after all to personality. The very fact that he is in a position to choose his family is something which would have appealed to the youth he was. Being without commitments and responsibilities is another aspect which young Jacques would have liked. Finally the callousness with which he treats his family is definitely reminiscent of what we have heard of the young Jacques. Gaston is the same person he was, but he is now in a more powerful position.
25. Anouilh, *Pièces noires*, 300.
26. *Ibid.*, 348.
27. Marsh, 76.
28. Valentine notices this. Cf. *Pièces noires*, 327.
29. Anouilh, *Nouvelles Pièces noires*, 185.
30. Cf. Hubert Gignoux, *Jean Anouilh*, 103.
31. Anouilh, *Nouvelles Pièces noires*, 193.
32. *Ibid.*, 135.
33. *Ibid.*, 166.

## CHAPTER V

1. Giraudoux, *Choix des élues*, 279.
2. Magny, 103.
3. Giraudoux, *Electre*, 39 f. Tr. by Winifred Smith in Bentley, *The Modern Theatre*, vol 1, 210. All translations by Winifred Smith are indicated in footnotes.
4. Cf. Sorensen, 206.
5. For a detailed description of "le destin" see the chapters in Jacques Houlet's *Le Théâtre de Giraudoux* and Sorensen's book of the same title, concerned with this problem. Houlet is the more verbose; Sorensen, the more penetrating and accurate.
6. Giraudoux, *Théâtre complet*, II, 14.
7. *Ibid.*, II, 35.
8. *Ibid.*, II, 92.
9. *Ibid.*, II, 101.
10. Cf. Houlet, 38.
11. Giraudoux, *Intermezzo*, 19.
12. *Ibid.*, 111 f.
13. *Ibid.*, 116.
14. *Ibid.*, 195.
15. Cf. Houlet, 97.
16. Giraudoux, *Electre*, 29. Tr. by Winifred Smith, 205.
17. *Ibid.*, 45. Tr. by Winifred Smith, 212.
18. *Ibid.*, 66.
19. *Ibid,*, 110 Tr. by Winifred Smith, 242.
20. *Ibid.*, 110 f. Tr. by Winifred Smith, 242.
21. *Ibid.*, 147.
22. *Ibid.*, 190. Tr. by Winifred Smith, 275.
23. *Ibid.*, 199.
24. Cf. Sorensen, 115.
25. Giraudoux, *Electre*, 225 ff. Tr. by Winifred Smith, 290-91.
26. Sorensen, 120.
27. Giraudoux, *Electre*, 219.
28. *Ibid.*, 227.
29. Giraudoux, *Ondine*, 226.
30. Giraudoux, *Intermezzo*, 210.
31. Giraudoux, *Théâtre complet*, X, 164.
32. Georges May, in an article in *Yale French Studies* (Fifth issue, p. 96), speaks of Giraudoux's heroes as being expert at beating the gods even when they seem to be defeated by them. But fate or destiny always wins in the end and seldom does man defeat it. Alcmène defeats Jupiter and becomes the symbol of conjugal fidelity, and Isabelle is brought back to reality. But Alcmène still has been seduced by Jupiter and will have Hercules to prove it. Does the god not have the last laugh? He has had his way after all. Isabelle does not defeat destiny; the Contrôleur does,

yet Isabelle is the heroine of the play. God triumphs over Judith because he plays on her pride and convinces her to become a saint. Electre, as an agent of fate, causes the ruin of her city, various murders, and her brother's madness. Ondine loses both herself and Hans. Sodom and Gomorrah are destroyed. These are hardly optimistic endings, and in each case the gods have the last laugh even if men put up a valiant fight against them.

33. Giraudoux, *Ondine*, 193 f.

34. *Ibid.*, 28.

35. *Ibid.*, 59.

36. *Ibid.*, 57.

37. *Ibid.*, 73.

38. This is exactly Lia's complaint against Jean in *Sodome et Gomorrhe*.

39. Giraudoux, *Ondine*, 146.

40. Cf. Houlet, 101.

41. Electre is as implacable in her way in her search for truth and justice as the king of the Ondins is in his. Because of an injustice seven years before, Argos is destroyed. Because of a pact made several years before, Hans dies. Electre and the king triumph and right wrongs.

42. Giraudoux, *Ondine*, 141.

43. Judith and Electre are exiles because *le destin* has made them so.

44. Giraudoux, *Théâtre complet*, X, 28 f.

45. *Ibid.*, X, 45.

46. *Ibid.*, X, 52.

47. *Ibid.*, X, 80.

48. *Ibid.*, X, 123.

49. *Ibid.*, X, 162.

# CHAPTER VI

1. Bentley, *The Playwright as Thinker*, 170.

2. Sartre, *Théâtre*, 24

3. *Ibid.*, 23.

4. *Ibid.*, 24.

5. *Ibid.*, 59.

6. *Ibid.*, 84.

7. By committing the murders he is in the same position as Egisthe was fifteen years before when he murdered Agamemnon, and by parallel the people of the town should share in his crime.

8. Sartre, *Théâtre*, 102.

9. Bentley, *The Playwright as Thinker*, 175.

10. Sartre, *Théâtre*, 185.

11. *Ibid.*, 187.

12. *Ibid.*, 198.

13. This is reminiscent of Garcin's trying to convince Inès (and himself) that he is not a coward.

14. Bentley, *The Playwright as Thinker*, 180.

15. Sartre, *Les Mains sales*, 98.

16. *Ibid.*, 100.

17. *Ibid.*, 210.

18. Sartre, *Théâtre*, 64.

19. Sartre, *Les Mains sales*, 247 f.

20. Cf. Sartre, *Le Diable et le bon Dieu*, statement on back cover.

21. *Ibid.*, 45 f.

22. *Ibid.*, 114 f.

23. *Ibid.*, 119.

24. *Ibid.*, 267.

25. *Ibid.*, 278.

26. *Ibid.*, 161 f.

27. *Ibid.*, 265.

28. Camus, *Le Malentendu, Caligula*, 110.

29. Camus, *Le Mythe de Sisyphe*, 38.

30. Camus, *Caligula*, 189.

31. *Ibid.*, 211.

32. Camus, *Le Mythe de Sisyphe*, 76 f.

# Bibliography

Albérès, René. *L'Aventure intéllectuelle du XX siècle*—1900-1950. Paris: La Nouvelle Edition, 1950.

—————. *La Révolte des écrivains d'aujourd'hui*. Paris: Editions Correa, 1949.

Aldridge, John. *After the Lost Generation*. New York: McGraw-Hill, 1951.

Amiel, Denys and André Obey. *La Souriante Mme Beudet, Théâtre*. Paris: A. Michel, 1926.

Anderson, Robert. *Tea and Sympathy*. New York: Random House, 1953.

Anouilh, Jean. *Ardèle ou la marguerite*. Paris: La Table Ronde, 1949.

—————. *Nouvelles Pièces noires*. Paris: La Table Ronde, 1946.

—————. *Pièces brillantes*. Paris: La Table Ronde, 1951.

—————. *Pièces noires*. Paris: Calmann-Lévy, 1942.

—————. *Pièces roses*. Paris: Calmann-Lévy, 1942.

—————. *La Valse des toréadors*. Paris: La Table Ronde, 1952.

—————. *Y Avait un prisonnier*. Paris: L,Illustration, 1935.

Augier, Emile. *Le Mariage d'Olympe, in Augier's Théâtre complet*, III. Paris: Calmann-Lévy, 1882-1884.

Balzac, Honoré de. *Cousine Bette*, in Balzac's *Oeuvres complètes*, XXVIII. Paris: Calmann-Lévy, 1891-1892.

Bendz, Ernest. "Le Désespoir dans l'oeuvre récente de Montherlant," in Michel de Saint-Pierre, *Montherlant, Bourreau de soi-même*. Paris: Gallimard, 1949.

Bentley, Eric. *In Search of Theatre*. New York: Knopf, 1953.

—————. *The Modern Theatre*, vol. 1. New York: Doubleday, 1955.

—————. *The Playwright as Thinker*. New York: Harcourt, Brace, 1949.

Bernard, Jean-Jacques. *L'Invitation au voyage, Théâtre*. Paris: A. Michel, 1925.

——————. *Martine, Théâtre*. Paris: A. Michel, 1925.

Blanchart, Paul. *Le Théâtre de Lenormand*. Paris: Masques, 1947.

Bourdet, Edouard. *La Fleur des pois*. Paris: Librairie Stock, 1933.

——————. *La Prisonnière*. Paris: Librairie Théâtrale, 1926.

——————. *Le Sexe faible*. Paris: Stock, 1931.

——————. *Les Temps difficiles*. Paris: L'Illustration, 1934.

Brieux, Eugène. *Théâtre complet*, 5 vols. Paris: Librairie Stock, 1923-1930.

Brisson, Pierre. *Le Thèâtre des Années Folles*. Genève: Ed. Du Milieu du Monde, 1943.

——————. *Du Meilleur au pire*. Paris: Gallimard, 1937.

Brodin, Pierre. *Les Ecrivains français de l'entre-deux guerres*. Montréal: Valiquette, 1945.

Campbell, Robert. *Jean-Paul Sartre*. Paris: Ed. Pierre Ardent, 1947.

Camus, Albert. *Caligula*. Paris: Gallimard, 1947.

——————. *Le Malentendu*. Paris: Gallimard, 1947.

——————. *Le Mythe de Sisyphe*. Paris: *Gallimard*, 1958.

Carot, Jacques. "Délivrance d'Anouilh," *Paru*, no. 29. Paris: Avril, 1947.

Cocteau, Jean. *Bacchus*. Paris: Gallimard, 1952.

——————. *Orphée*. Paris: Stock, 1927.

Cory, Daniel Webster. *The Homosexual in America*. New York: Greenberg, 1951.

Crommelynck, Fernand. *Le Cocu magnifique*. Paris: Editions Emile-Paul frères, 1931.

Curel, François de. *Les Fossiles*, in *Théâtre complet*, II. Paris: Crès, 1920.

Didier, Jean. *A la rencontre de Jean Anouilh*. Paris: Ed. de la Sixaine, 1946.

Dumas, fils, Alexandre. *La Dame au camélias*, in *Théâtre complet*, I. Paris: Michel Lévy, 1906-1910.

Falize, Jean. *A la Rencontre de Jean Giraudoux*. Paris: La Sixaine, 1946.

Gide, André. *Corydon*. Paris: Gallimard, 1947.

——————. *Les Faux-Monnayeurs*. Paris: Gallimard, 1943.

——————. *Journal*. Paris: N. R. F., 1939.

——————. *Journals*, tr. by Justin O'Brien. New York: Knopf, 1949.

——————. *Et nunc manet in te*. Neuchâtel et Paris: Ides et Calendes, 1951.

——— ———. *Si le grain ne meurt*. Paris: Gallimard, 1939.

Gignoux, Hubert. *Jean Anouilh*. Paris: Editions du Temps Présent, 1946.

Giraudoux, Jean. *Choix des élues*. Paris: Grasset. 1939.

----------. *Electre*. Paris: Grasset, 1937.

----------. *La Folle de Chaillot*. Paris: Grasset, 1946.

----------. *Intermezzo*. Paris: Grasset, 1933.

----------. *Littérature*. Paris: Grasset, 1941.

----------. *Ondine*. Paris: Grasset, 1939.

----------. *Pour Lucrèce*. Paris: Grasset, 1953.

----------. *Théâtre complet*, 15 vols. Neuchâtel et Paris: Ides et Calendes. 1945-48.

Green, Julien. *Sud*. Paris: Plon, 1953.

Grube, G. M. A. *The Drama of Euripides*. London: Methuen, 1941.

Hadas, Moses. *History of Greek Literature*. New York: Columbia University Press, 1950.

Hellman, Lillian. *The Children's Hour*, in *Four Plays*, by Lillian Hellman. New York: The Modern Library, n.d.

Houlet, Jacques. *Le Théâtre de Jean Giraudoux*. Paris: Ed. Pierre Ardent, 1945.

Jaccard, Pierre. *Trois Contemporains*. Lausanne: Ed. La Concorde, 1945.

James, Henry. *Great Short Novels*, ed. Philip Rahv. New York: Dial Press, 1945.

Krutch, Joseph Wood. *The Modern Temper*. New York: Harcourt, Brace, 1929.

----------. *Modernism in the Modern Drama*. Ithaca: Cornell University Press, 1953.

Lalou, René. *Roger Martin du Gard*. Paris: Gallimard, 1938.

LaPrade, Jacques de. *Le Théâtre de Montherlant*. Paris: La Jeune Parque, 1950.

Lavedan, Henri. *Le Marquis de Priola*. Paris: Flammarion, 1902.

Lenormand, Henri-René. *Confessions d'un auteur dramatique*, 2 vols. Paris: Albin Michel, 1949.

----------. *Théâtre complet*, 10 vols. Paris: Albin Michel, 1925-1949.

Magny, Claude-Edmonde. *Précieux Giraudoux*. Paris: Ed. du Seuil, 1945.

Mann, Thomas. *The Thomas Mann Reader*, sel., arr., & ed. by J. W. Angell. New York: Knopf, 1950.

Marsh, Edward Owen, *Jean Anouilh: Poet of Pierrot and Pantaloon*. London: W. H. Allen & Co., 1953.

Martin du Gard, Roger. *Un Taciturne*. Paris: Gallimard, 1932.

May, Georges. "Jean Giraudoux: Diplomacy and Dramaturgy," *Yale French Studies*, No. 5. New Haven: Payne and Lane, 1950.

Montherlant, Henri de. *Les Célibataires*. Paris: Grasset, 1934.

----------. *Service inutile*. Paris: Grasset, 1935.

——————. *Textes sous une occupation*. Paris: Gallimard, 1953.

——————. *Théâtre complet*, 6 vols. Paris et Neuchâtel: Ides et Calendes, 1950-1951.

——————. *La Ville dont le prince est un enfant*. Paris: Gallimard, 1951.

Morand, Paul. "Armance ne rime peut-être pas avec Impuissance," *La Nouvelle Nouvelle Revue Française*, Mai, 1953.

Norwood, Gilbert. *Greek Tragedy*. London: Methuen, 1920.

O'Neill, Eugene. *Nine Plays*. New York: Modern Library, 1941.

Peyre, Henri. *The Contemporary French Novel*. New York: Oxford University Press, 1955.

Praz, Mario. *The Romantic Agony*. London: Oxford University Press, 1951.

Proust, Marcel. *A la recherche du temps perdu*. Paris: Gallimard, 1945.

Radine, Serge. *Anouilh, Lenormand, Salacrou*. Genève: Editions des Trois Collines, 1951.

Rops, Daniel. *Sur le théâtre de Lenormand*. Paris: Editions des Cahiers Libres, 1926.

Rousseau, Jean Jacques. *Les Confessions*, in *Oeuvres Complètes*, XIV. Paris: Du Pont, 1823-1824.

Saint-Pierre, Michel de. *Montherlant, Bourreau de soi-même*. Paris: Gallimard, 1949.

Sartre, Jean-Paul. *Le Diable et le bon Dieu*. Paris: Gallimard, 1951.

——————. *L'Existentialisme est un humanisme*. Paris: Les Editions Nagel, 1946.

——————. *Les Mains sales*. Paris: Gallimard, 1947.

——————. *Situations*, 2 vols. Paris: Gallimard, 1947-1948.

——————. *Théâtre*. Paris: Gallimard, 1947.

Shairp, Mordaunt. *The Green Bay Tree*, in *Sixteen Famous British Plays*, ed. by B. A. Cerf and Van Cartmell. New York: Modern Library, 1942.

Siepmann, E. O. "The New Pessimism in France," *The Nineteenth Century and After*. May, 1948.

Simon, Pierre-Henri. *Procès du héros*. Paris: Editions du Seuil, 1950.

——————. *Témoins de l'homme*. Paris: Librairie Armand Colin, 1951.

Sophocles. *Plays and Fragments*, 2 vols., ed. Lewis Campbell. London: Oxford, 1881.

Sorensen, Hans. *Le Théâtre de Jean Giraudoux*. Copenhagen: Universitet-sforlaget i Aarhus Ejnar Munksgaard, 1950.

Truc, Gonzague. *De Sartre à Lavalle*. Paris: Tissot, 1946.

Van Nuffell, Robert O. J. "Jean Anouilh," *Rivista di Letterature Moderne*, anno III. Marzogiugno, 1948.

Vildrac, Charles. *Le Paquebot Tenacity*, in *Representative Plays from the French Theatre of Today*, ed. Hélène Harvitt. Boston: Heath, 1940.

——————. *Le Pèlerin*, with *Michel Auclair*. Paris: Gallimard, 1923.

Voltaire, François Marie Arouet de. *Dictionnaire philosophique*, 2 vols. Paris: Garnier, 1946-1947.

Westwood, Gordon. *Society and the Homosexual*. New York: E. P. Dutton, 1953.

Williams, Tennessee. *Camino Real*. Norfolk: New Directions, 1953.

——————. *A Streetcar Named Desire*. New York: New Directions, 1st printing, 1947.

# Index